trotman

What can I do with... an arts degree?

2nd edition

Gill Sharp & Beryl Dixon

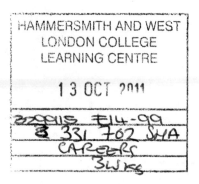
What can I do with . . . an arts degree?

This second edition is published in 2009 by Trotman Publishing, an imprint of
Crimson Publishing, Westminster House, Kew Road, Richmond, Surrey TW9 2ND.

© Trotman Publishing 2009

Authors: Gill Sharp & Beryl Dixon

First edition by Beryl Dixon and published in 2002 by Trotman and Company Ltd
© Trotman and Company Ltd

All data from the report 'What do graduates do?' is included with the permission of
AGCAS and HECSU. For the latest version of this publication, see www.prospects.
ac.uk. For permission to reproduce, contact copyright@agcas.org.uk and copyright@
prospects.ac.uk.

ISBN 978-1-84455-210-8

British Library Cataloguing in Publication Data
A catalogue record for this book is available from the British Library

Typeset by IDSUK (DataConnection) Ltd.

Printed and bound in Italy by LEGO SpA

Contents

About the Authors

GILL SHARP

Gill Sharp is a freelance careers adviser and writer. She is also a partner in Domino Careers (www.dominocareers.co.uk) an internet and telephone-based career consultancy.

BERYL DIXON

Is an experienced carers adviser who has worked in different careers companies and in a tertiary college where she advised students of all ages on employment and higher education choices. She now concentrates on careers writing and is the author of several books on careers and higher education.

Acknowledgements

I hope you enjoy reading this book as much as I enjoyed researching it. Let me thank all those who helped me with my background investigations: the Careers Group, University of London; the Career Development Services at the University of Wales Institute, Cardiff; Creative Careers at the University of the Arts, London; Liz Hagger at Domino Careers; the Centre for Career and Personal Development at Canterbury Christ Church University; Palatine at Lancaster University; the alumni association of the University of Gloucestershire; all the employers who contributed their time so generously; and most of all, my case studies.

Gill Sharp

I would like to thank Clare Wright of Birmingham University Careers Advisory Service, Jeff Goodman of Bristol University Careers Advisory Service, Kevin Thomson of Reading University Careers Advisory Service, Claire Reed of York University Careers Advisory Service and Carl Gilleard, Chief Executive of Graduate Recruiters, for their assistance when I was researching this book.

Beryl Dixon

Introduction

Approximately 40% of the 18-plus age group now go through higher education. What are the benefits of higher education? Why should so many young people do degrees, especially as it involves a major investment of time and money?

The most obvious benefit is financial. Graduates as a group are paid more than those who have not attended university, both at the start of their career and as they progress through the ranks. Naturally, pay varies between sectors and is subject to economic fluctuations. In 2008, the latest year for which data is available, the median starting salary for a graduate was approximately £24,500, with some lucky recruits in law and banking/finance being paid in excess of £35,000.* Don't forget, though, that that is the median. If some are earning £36,000+, others are earning around £11,000 or less. But these are people at the very start of their careers and their chance to obtain much higher monetary rewards is good whatever the sector in which they begin their professional life.

So what are the key trends in careers? There is a growing interest in and expansion of work in the cultural, artistic, environmental and charity/international development areas. None of these is likely to provide graduates with the highest possible financial benefits, but this is not the sole reason for entry into many careers.

Do graduates automatically find more interesting jobs than non-graduates? With an ever-increasing number of students going on to higher education there is more competition for top posts. And what exactly is a graduate job? Certainly some graduates are doing jobs that would once have been done by 18-year-old or even 16-year-old entrants. Some

---

Source: Association of Graduate Recruiters, Graduate Recruitment Survey, summer review 2008.

complain that their ability is under-utilised. On the other hand, many employers want more highly educated people who can introduce change and make things happen.

Students are often dissuaded from doing an arts (or humanities) degree because it is not seen as leading to any particular career. However, the array of work done by the graduates featured in this book shows the range of possibilities – as long as you are proactive and highly motivated.

AROUND 40% OF JOBS ADVERTISED FOR GRADUATES DO NOT SPECIFY A DEGREE SUBJECT

The main benefit of higher education is that graduates should gain key skills that are valued by employers. A degree alone is no guarantee of a job and nor is an outstanding class of degree. Charlotte Driscoll in Chapter 6, for instance, gained a First but still needed to attend approximately 20 interviews before finding her first post. Luck, stamina, energy and perseverance have a part to play, whoever you are and whatever your grades. More important than in-depth knowledge of ancient Rome or Milton's sonnets is your general level of ability and your transferable skills (i.e. those that can be used in any job). A student with a First in history, who has spent three years sitting in the library, is not sought after by too many employers. A student with a 2.i who has taken part in a range of extra-curricular activities and had a part-time job is a much better prospect.

Do not think that certain careers automatically require degrees in certain subjects. What can be done by a historian should be equally possible for a modern linguist or classics graduate: here, as well as more 'conventional' options, we have a classicist who became an actor, a drama graduate and a historian who work in TV production, a fine artist who manages a wildlife charity, a classical music graduate who is a technical writer and former philosophy students who work in marketing, branding and advertising. We consider 'typical' and 'non-typical' career paths and the increasing crossover between disciplines and sectors. So don't just look at your subject or the career area that specifically interests you. Once you have read about these, see where other arts graduates have begun their careers and learn from their experiences in jobs that you may have dismissed and others that you may not have heard of.

It is prospective arts graduates who most frequently ask 'What could I do with philosophy?' or 'Where would history lead me?' Read on! If you are planning to take an arts degree or are already on an arts course at university, this book is for you.

A NOTE ON THE EMPLOYMENT STATISTICS USED IN THIS BOOK

Some chapters include data from the Higher Education Statistics Agency (HESA), which provides detailed analysis of careers entered by graduates in different subjects and disciplines from data supplied to them by universities and colleges. The latest figures at the time of writing are for 2007. They are published by the Higher Education Careers Services Unit (HECSU) under the title 'What do graduates do' and are based on information supplied by graduates themselves. However, these figures should be treated with caution. Compiled six months after most students graduate, they are bound to include some who are in temporary jobs while making applications for 'graduate-level' jobs.

1 Myths and Facts About Where an Arts Degree Can Lead

POSSIBLE CAREER PATHS FOR ART GRADUATES

So just what can you do with an arts degree? Unless you re-train virtually from scratch, you cannot become an engineer, architect, doctor, pharmacist, rocket scientist – or a host of other things for which a vocational degree and professional training are prerequisites. But that still leaves a lot. Try to think beyond the obvious and don't make any assumptions about what an arts degree can lead to or preclude. The following professions are all possibilities, whatever subject you study:

- Accountancy
- Administration
- Advertising
- Air force
- Air traffic control
- Army
- Arts administration
- Auctioneering and valuing
- Bank management
- Bookselling
- Building society management
- Buying
- Careers advice
- Charity work
- Civil service
- Company secretaryship
- Computer programming
- Conference and/or events management
- Customs and excise
- Diplomacy
- Estate agents
- Financial advice
- Freight forwarding
- Health service management
- Hotel management
- Housing management
- Human resources
- Immigration
- Information management/ science
- IT consultancy
- Journalism
- Law
- Librarianship
- Local government
- Logistics management
- Loss adjusting
- Management consultancy
- Market research
- Marketing
- Merchant navy

- Museum work
- Police
- Prison services
- Probation services
- Public relations
- Publishing
- Purchasing
- Recruitment
- Retail management
- Royal Marines
- Royal Navy
- Social work/services
- Tourism
- Training
- Web design
- Youth and community work.

For some careers a postgraduate qualification is essential – irrespective of first-degree subject:

- Barrister
- Librarian
- Probation officer
- Social worker
- Solicitor
- Surveyor
- Teacher (in a state school, and increasingly in publicly funded further and higher education).

In other careers, completion of a postgraduate course may help to gain entry where there is competition for jobs.

All graduates should be aware that study does not always end in a degree. Would-be accountants, for example, learn while doing the job but have to work in their spare time towards professional examinations set by the different accountancy bodies. Only when they pass these exams do they become fully qualified. In other careers, qualifications exist but are optional. Having said that, many employers will expect graduates to obtain these, e.g. newspaper editors will expect trainee journalists to obtain the National Council for the Training of Journalists' qualifications, and most organisations would want their human resources staff to become qualified through the Chartered Institute of Personnel and Development.

You do not always have to do a full-time course and find the necessary tuition fees. Many relevant qualifications may be done on a part-time basis while you work in an unrelated job to keep body and soul together. Distance learning and e-learning are now widely available. You can find much of the information you need on entry and training routes on various careers websites and reference books. For suggested links and titles, see Chapter 16.

Myth

- Arts graduates become teachers, usually in the secondary school system.
- Arts graduates are unemployable.
- Arts graduates are limited to a very narrow range of careers according to the subject they have studied. (English graduates all go into publishing or journalism; historians into archiving or museum work.)
- In today's crowded job market, a master's degree is needed to get on.
- An MA, or, even better, a PhD, will set you apart from the crowd and enhance your job and pay prospects.
- A master's is a good way of buying time and possibly compensating for a disappointing bachelor's degree result.

Fact

- Between 35% and 40% of jobs advertised for graduates do not require a degree in a specific subject.
- Only a few of the case studies in this book are involved in education and just two are teachers.
- Arts graduates have a general level of ability and certain skills valued by employers. All of our case studies are a testimony to the fact that arts graduates can survive and thrive in a huge range of occupations.
- Many people doing the same jobs have degrees in English, history, music or even chemistry or engineering. Further study is often required to gain professional qualifications.
- Many employers welcome second degrees, as they prove that you can cope with a rigorous intellectual regime. Nowadays, a lot of vocational courses such as those aimed at social work, human resources or marketing allow you to gain a master's as well as a job-specific qualification. Those that don't, i.e. those that are purely academic, rarely suffice;

recruiters also want to see relevant work experience. With more and more people taking masters' courses they may no longer differentiate you in the way that they did even a few years ago. In some cases a diploma or certificate is seen as a good substitute for an MA – it may even be valued more highly because it is focused and practical rather than just theoretical.

■ Higher degrees in the arts and humanities aren't treated in quite the same way as those in the sciences, where they are often a requirement for entry to certain jobs. Those who have done further study in arts subjects are considered alongside applicants with bachelor's level education; it is up to them to market their skills, experience and knowledge on an individual basis.

■ The best – some would say the only – reason for doing an MA is to pursue the subject for its own sake. More and more students are undertaking postgraduate study, but not always for the right reasons. It is an expensive stop-gap if you don't enjoy the course or if it gets you no further forward with your career plans. As for making up for a disappointing degree classification, employers will always look back to your original grades (and sometimes to your A level/Highers and International Baccalaureate (IB) passes too.) So think carefully before enrolling on an MA: it is not a universal solution.

WHAT IF YOU HAVE A 2.I OR A 2.II?

A 2.ii may hold you back a little when looking for work, but most people find ways around it. Several of our case studies have demonstrated that the world doesn't stop if you miss out on a 2.i. And once you have secured a first job, no one will ever ask about your class of degree again.

Myth

■ The majority of graduates go onto prestigious training schemes with large companies – as long as they have a 2.i and a relevant degree.

Fact

- Less than 15% of all graduates take part in a graduate programme of this type: places are limited and even high flyers sometimes miss out – particularly the first time around. These are run by very few employers, mainly in the private sector, although the Civil Service, the National Health Service (NHS) and local government are among the public sector organisations with large schemes of this type.
- A 2.i is often a prerequisite, but not all employers disbar those with a 2.ii degree. Be selective if you have a lower second: contact the recruitment department if you feel that there were mitigating factors surrounding your result and also highlight any relevant skills and experience you have. Ask if they will consider you. What do you have to lose?
- The majority of graduate schemes will consider graduates of any discipline, though some may specify certain skills or academic disciplines. Even these may not be set in stone. One English graduate talked her way into an interview for fashion buying, which asked for a business or art degree. How did she do it? By stressing her background in retail, having worked in a major store since the age of 16. She played her trump card by talking about her dissertation – which centred on the use of clothing and fabrics in the novels of a major Victorian writer.

NEW WAYS OF WORKING

Let's challenge the received wisdom that you will be employed in just one sector all your life. It is likely that today's graduates will have, on average, three major career switches before they retire.

In the 21st century, working 9–5, Monday to Friday, for just one employer is no longer the only possibility open to graduates, particularly those studying arts subjects. They may, out of choice of necessity, be 'portfolio' workers, doing a range of different jobs with several employers according to the time of year or the day of the week: Jamie MacCarthy provides an insider's view of this type of workstyle in Chapter 6, as does

Lindsey Ashwin in Chapter 11. Also in Chapter 6, Stacey McIntosh reflects on serial redundancy: this is one of the hidden hazards of a career in the media, not just in his own sector (journalism) but in film, broadcasting and advertising too.

The alternative to the above could be to setting up in business by yourself or working as a consultant. Self-employment now accounts for 34% of all recent graduates in the creative industries (visual arts, performing arts, media, sports and cultural activities). With successive governments advocating entrepreneurship and backing this up with practical support, the figure is likely to increase and extend into other professions.

Self-employment

Many university leavers, particularly in the arts, dislike the idea of reporting to an employer and/or want to do something creative of their own. Jim Lockey is a recent graduate of the popular music course at the University of Gloucestershire, and he has taken the bold step of setting up in business with his own record label called *Istartedthefire*, promoting indie folk music and related artists. Jim is the director and has friends working with him. He thinks that his degree gave him a good start, but it has been a steep learning curve: '*My course was a great introduction to the industry, because it gave us an inside view of how it works. It also helped us all to find out where we stood with regard to legalities, contracts and having the right procedure in place. Without that, a lot of start-up businesses get into trouble.*'

Jim had wanted to do this almost since starting university: he leads a band called Jim Lockey and the Solemn Sun and found his artists in local venues and student gigs around the Cheltenham area. '*In that sense it was easy because we all support each other and there's a family ethos to the whole venture.*'

However, there are pitfalls: although Jim knew a fair amount about the music business, he realised that his knowledge of the wider business world was lacking. He contacted Companies House, a government department that can advise and register commercial enterprises, and Business

Link, which provides help – and sometimes funding – for the self-employed and entrepreneurs. Jim found both organisations very helpful. *'They told us everything we need to know, including the importance of becoming a limited company, which protects us if things don't go to plan. Now we're waiting to hear from the Inland Revenue and make our first tax return!'*

Jim appreciates that the newly self-employed may have to wait some while before their business makes any substantial profit: he reckons as long as three to five years is a realistic timescale. *'There's no instant income and we are dependent on the sale of our products. We send these to a distributor, they place them in stores and shops and then these retail outlets sell them. We don't get any money until that happens.'*

While waiting for *Istartedthefire* to take off, Jim and his colleagues have other casual jobs to pay the rent.

'This is something I always wanted to do and although I tried to talk myself out of it, the reward is that I'm doing something that I love. I'd recommend anyone else who's thinking of setting up in business to seek advice, take the plunge and have faith!'

Freelancing

Another mode of work is freelancing with a number of finite contracts or moving from one freelance employer to another rather than being permanently employed. Dan Grey, a well-established and successful assistant TV producer, describes this way of life:

'The key thing is that it's not secure, which can be uncomfortable at times, particularly over Christmas and when the country as a whole is going through a lean period. I went on holiday thinking I could come back and pick up work as I had done before and really got a wake up call when I couldn't find anything. But I have other skills and have kept myself afloat thorough temp clerical employment, though I wasn't making the sort of salary I'd become used to. It certainly will be tricky if I ever want a mortgage – that could be scary.'

Any other drawbacks? '*You don't get the perks and bonuses that a permanent job attracts and if you do take time off you won't be paid, so you need to factor that in before booking a vacation!*'

What are the plus points? '*Constant change and variety. I've been able to travel with my job to the States and the Caribbean. I love doing projects, making friends, enjoying new experiences, then moving on.*'

Read more about Dan's career in Chapter 12.

Shifting structures

Even if you prefer more conventional working patterns, the old order is changing. The traditional structure contains jobs in which, as a manager, you would be in charge of a team of people and be responsible for their work. In turn you would report to someone more senior. Eventually you would hope for promotion and a range of increasingly senior jobs. However, managers do not merely supervise and carry out instructions. They are expected to think, come up with ideas and contribute to their workplace's development.

This framework still prevails, but it exists alongside other systems. In many organisations, particularly in the consultancy, IT, financial and communications industries, teams are formed to work on individual projects. When it ends, the members leave to begin different projects. You might work with some of the same people again; with others, never. Teams and team roles may even change during the course of a project. The ability to form working relationships quickly is crucial in this kind of employment.

In other workplaces, there may be no hierarchical structure or linear progression. Promotion and other opportunities may be random – a case of 'blink or you'll miss it' – and also a product of working hard, being open to acquiring new skills and carving a niche for yourself. There is a move away from specialisation, particularly at the beginning of your career. Most recruiters who take on university leavers want someone prepared to get involved in a range of areas and to multi-task. This is true of both big corporations and small to medium-sized enterprises (SMEs). The latter are relative newcomers to graduate recruitment but are making an increasing contribution to the economy and to the graduate labour market.

This is lot to take on board when you are planning your career, but factor all this information into your research. The next chapter looks at yet another piece of the jigsaw: 'What do employers want?'

2 What Do Employers Want?

Why do companies employ graduates? As mentioned earlier, as far as arts graduates are concerned it is rarely for your specific subject knowledge. Rather it is because studying an academic subject at degree level has given you certain intellectual skills plus a level of personal maturity. Arts graduates can:

- **reason** – they learn to form their own opinions without a 'set in stone' correct answer
- **analyse** – before they can present their case they have to assess and evaluate information
- **communicate** – on most arts courses, students give presentations, either individually or in a team. They lead discussions and respond to comments from staff and classmates. They have to defend their views under pressure. Hopefully they also learn to listen to other people and accept their points of view. ('Active' listening is an important part of communication.) Students in the performing and visual arts also have to take on board others' evaluations of their work and learn to use criticism to enhance their professional development
- **take responsibility for their own learning** and **manage their time** – seven or eight hours of lectures each week means that eventually most students learn the arts of self-discipline and time management. These skills, however, are not enough to guarantee an interesting job. They must be allied to what most recruiters call transferable or key skills.

Communication is one of the top attributes sought by graduate recruiters. This is closely followed by several other skills that are common to nearly all employers, regardless of their line of business:

- adaptability
- client care and customer orientation
- commercial awareness
- commitment
- communication, both oral and written
- computer literacy
- initiative, resourcefulness and drive
- languages
- leadership
- networking
- numeracy
- persistence and ambition
- persuasive powers
- planning, prioritising and decision making
- problem-solving ability
- self-awareness
- self-reliance
- teamwork
- willingness to learn.

WHAT DO SOME OF THESE SKILLS MEAN IN THE EMPLOYMENT CONTEXT?

Adaptability

No job stays the same for long. Almost certainly you will have to constantly update your skills and acquire new ones as your professional sector changes. You will work with new technology and keep abreast of this. You will also be operating in a global economy. This may mean that, like several of our case studies, you are travelling beyond the UK or liaising with colleagues and clients across the world. At the very minimum, it supposes that you will be aware of social, political and cultural considerations in the UK and further afield. All this demands a flexible attitude.

Commercial awareness

If private sector businesses don't make profits, they fail; the public sector has tight budgets to meet and is more and more preoccupied with generating income. This is also the case in the 'third sector' – charities and non-governmental organisations (NGOs), where there is a need for people who understand how to raise funds and bring sponsors on board. Employers always look to increase their income and decrease their costs. Graduates need to understand the implications of this.

Communication

At work you must communicate with colleagues and possibly with customers and suppliers. You might have to supervise or manage junior staff. You will almost certainly have to produce written reports and documents, bids for money or resources and give PowerPoint presentations. You might have to explain things to people who do not share your level of knowledge.

You will have to be able to present yourself in a business-like way, however demanding the circumstances, and also to socialise professionally. A common complaint from employers is that new graduates cannot make small talk with clients or consumers.

Electronic communication is another potential minefield. We routinely dash off phone calls, texts and emails to our nearest and dearest, but there is an etiquette to doing this in a work context. Then there will be meetings. Your arguments must be rehearsed, ready, foolproof – but ready to be adapted and restated if necessary. Meetings are the time to think on your feet.

Networking, both formal and informal, is becoming more prevalent as a method of accessing promotion posts, sideways moves and career transitions. This method of marketing yourself causes anxiety to some graduates, but it can be learned and is becoming an essential communication skill, as many of our case studies show.

Initiative

In most graduate jobs, employers want innovators with ideas, who will challenge the status quo and improve on it.

Leadership

This is not simply implementing a strategy by telling people what to do. They may need to be convinced, persuaded, helped. As team leader you must deploy your resources/staff as effectively as possible, playing to people's strengths, taking into account the ways in which they work best and addressing any shortcomings that might have a negative impact on the task in hand.

Numeracy

If you dropped maths with a sigh of relief after GCSE, remember that most jobs involve some numbers. There is a big difference, though, between understanding and feeling comfortable with figures, graphs and charts (numeracy) and the finer aspects of calculus, geometry and algebra (maths). If you are aiming at a big graduate employer it is likely that your aptitude with figures will be tested during the selection process.

Persuasive powers

Being able to get your own way through negotiation and diplomacy is a very valuable skill. You may use it in meeting sales targets or convincing sceptical potential clients and customers to commit to a particular course of action.

Problem-solving ability

At work you won't just have academic arguments to weigh up. There will be constraints due to budget problems, timescale or lack of employees with the right skills. Your solution may need a lot of adaptation and compromise, often under pressure.

Self-reliance

After initial training you will be expected to stand on your own feet and not need constant supervision. The skill in managing your own learning is in knowing at what point you need to ask for clarification or assistance.

Many employers now recruit graduates directly into specific jobs – and expect them to begin to contribute almost immediately. They are given real work to do while they gain their experience. There is consequently a need for graduates who can use their initiative and take charge of their own learning.

SOME EMPLOYERS' VIEWPOINTS
Procter & Gamble

Gareth Barker (whose case study is given in Chapter 13) does some graduate recruitment himself for his employers, Procter & Gamble. The company sells over 300 products, including brand-name cosmetics, household products and foods, in about 150 countries. It recruits graduates into a range of careers. Specific subject degrees are required for entry to research, development and product supply, but the following jobs are open to graduates in any discipline: customer business development, financial management, human resources, IT and Gareth's specialism, marketing.

Gareth says, 'We don't mind what type of degree you have – as long as it's a 2.i. Nor do we emphasise commercial experience. What we do seek is leadership qualities – it's the first thing that I look for and it's the number one most important quality for any type of marketing career. Team playing and collaboration are important, but we don't want people who just do what they're told. So whatever subject you're studying, throw yourself into some extra-curricular activities, whether it's in student societies or outside university, and develop your leadership and collaboration skills. When it comes to applications and interviews, we suggest that you remember the acronym CAR (context/action/ results) when providing examples. Always have three or four instances of killer evidence that show what YOU have done and that roll off the tongue. Talk about what specifically you did when you have been working in a team. It can feel a bit unnatural to "blow your own trumpet" as such, but we're really keen to understand specifically what you have achieved, and the type of role you take when in a team.'

Halcrow

Halcrow specialises in the provision of planning, design and management services for infrastructure development worldwide. With interests in transportation, water, maritime and property, the company is currently undertaking commissions in over 80 countries through a network of more than 90 offices.

Jade Clifford is UK recruitment team supervisor for the company, taking on many new graduates each year. She says to anyone with an arts degree that joining Halcrow will jumpstart their career and fast-track their progress in the professional realm. *'Our graduates' fresh perspectives and energy continually inspire us, and you'll be treated as an essential part of the team from the outset. Far from being trapped behind a photocopier, we want to hear what you have to say and your ideas for improving our business. You won't be dropped in the deep end – our mentoring schemes align you with our senior staff, providing you with a role model and someone to turn to with questions about your career choices. Because our way of working draws together a huge variety of disciplines – economists, architects, transport planners, ecologists and civil engineers might all collaborate on a project – you'll benefit from exposure to a broad mix of people, skills and methods.'*

The consulting business group is the main part of the company where Halcrow would be interested in hearing from arts graduates. It has two skill areas that would have the most relevant opportunities: economics and business solutions and transport planning.

So why might these opportunities be suitable for arts graduates? Jade highlights several reasons:

- *'we're interested in broadening our scope beyond engineering, scientific and mathematical degrees*
- *arts students have often used skills that would benefit our business, such as being analytical and having good problem-solving abilities*
- *many of the roles within our consulting business group are dealing with complex organisational problems, so although our clients are within infrastructure, they are still political, social, environmental and economical issues, for example revenue forecasting, appeasing public opinion, achieving our wider social aim.'*

Jade cites as one just one example of a successful arts
graduate in the business as a pedestrian modeller who has an
English degree. She looks for someone who:

- is enthusiastic
- is committed
- has good communication skills
- has good numeracy
- has good problem-solving skills
- is analytical.

Whitechapel Gallery

What if you want to do something more specific with your
degree or work for an SME?

Sarah Walsh is an arts administrator at Whitechapel
Gallery in London's East End. Herself an arts graduate, you
can find her case study in Chapter 4. Part of her current role
is human resources, so she is well used to receiving both
formal and speculative applications from university leavers.

'In terms of skills, we need strong organisational ability,
time management and evidence of being able to hit tight
deadlines. Most people develop these as part of their degree,
but there are things that you can do beyond your course that
will make you even more employable. Apart from voluntary
work and internships, you could coordinate an exhibition
with friends, for instance, or run an arts event.'

She also points out the importance of being computer
literate. 'Most jobs in the arts will involve using IT – Excel
spreadsheets to sort out budgets, databases for mailing lists.
We would expect you to be able to use those types of basic
applications.'

Communication also ranks highly on Sarah's list of desirable
attributes. 'You should be friendly and willing to communicate
with pretty much everybody, within the organisation and
beyond it.' Further key assets are adaptability and enthusiasm.
'It's important to be able to work towards the common good
and also to be ready to develop new skills as and when they
are needed. In a small organisation particularly, this is vital,

because you just have to muck in. In a larger workplace
– and the gallery has recently increased its staff from 45
to 60 – you are more likely to find dedicated departments
that require specialised input. We have separate sections
for communications, exhibitions, education, development,
administration and finance, operations, visitor services and
the director's office. These all, too, have subdivisions and it's
worthwhile understanding this before you apply and showing
that knowledge in your CV.'

(Sarah discusses CVs in greater detail in Chapter 15.)

Start in TV

David Wheeler is Director of the recruitment website 'Start in
TV'. He has worked in TV and film for many years, so has a
great deal of insight into the skills necessary to begin a career
in the media industry. 'Principally what are needed are good
communicators and team players with enthusiasm and a can
do/will do attitude. You need to be sufficiently easy going
to get along with everybody that you meet and committed
enough to do even the most routine jobs to the best of your
ability. And alongside this you must have curiosity – by
which I mean being eager to learn, to listen, to absorb.'

David's own degree is in Chemistry – what does he
think arts graduates can offer? He flags up the fact that
broadcast/film media uses all the creative disciplines – design,
photography, writing, fine art and performance. 'It's likely that
people from that sort of background will have better written
and oral skills and be able to come up with ideas. They also
need discernment and judgement. A typical shoot may involve
days of filming for just an hour's worth of material. You need
to be able to know who to talk to, how to gather information
and images, then be able to sift and select what you need.'

SELECTION PROCEDURES

Selection procedures typically begin with an application
form, usually online. The forms usually include tricky
questions along the lines of the ones listed below.

- Describe a major achievement that you are proud of.
- Describe a problem or difficulty you have overcome and how.
- Give examples of occasions when you have used leadership skills.

Not exactly easy – but how do arts students spend a large proportion of their time if not in thinking, assessing, making notes and then presenting a case?

Many large companies and public sector employers have a selection process that consists of several phases. Students who pass the initial stage are invited to an assessment day(s), which consist of some or all of the following:

- written tests of verbal reasoning, numeracy and often personality
- group discussions
- individual presentations
- one-to-one interviews – often with several interviewers – and sometimes involving two or three interviews some weeks apart.

You may be asked to give a prepared presentation or deliver one on the spot. In small groups you might discuss a topic related to current affairs or an aspect of the work of the company. Recruiters observe and assess how well candidates are performing against a checklist of skills.

Smaller companies are more likely to rely on a CV followed by one or perhaps two interviews, possibly with a presentation thrown in for good measure. However, there is now a trend towards more complex application processes in the arts sector. Even a role as a box office administrator may attract hundreds of graduate applicants, who are therefore put through the same hoops as the ones described above.

NON-ACADEMIC SKILLS AND YOU

How can you acquire any missing skills?

Make a list of the skills you feel you need to acquire or brush up. Then try to hone these through extra-curricular activities and part-time/summer work. Higher education is not simply about getting a degree. It is about developing as a person. All those readily available and relatively cheap sports and leisure activities can positively add to your CV. Avoid a list of activities in which you were the passenger.

Do also make use of any opportunity to develop a wide range of interests. This will prove to potential employers that you can manage your time. (Here you are with a good class of degree and yet you also spent hours a week on the sports field, in the orchestra, not to mention the union bar. And you probably held down a part-time job as well. So, you aren't someone who is going to crack when asked to handle several problems at the same time or meet a tight deadline.)

Better still, make one of your interests a major one – and take a key part in organising it or contributing to it at university.

Adaptability

Any evidence that you like new environments or have travelled, worked or lived in different places will be an advantage. Modern linguists who have spent a period abroad, or students in other subjects who have done this through the ERASMUS programme or a gap year, can lay claim to the adaptability that this confers.

Communication

Don't hang back in seminars. Take every opportunity to give presentations. You could also get a student job in a shop, bar or telephone call centre – where talking to people is essential.

Initiative

Have you organised an event, started a club, led a team? Raised funds? Been responsible for implementing any change – from hall of residence menus to the course syllabus, through membership of relevant committees?

Leadership

Employers want people who could become managers. If you supervise or train other staff in your part-time job or if you are a sports team captain or class representative, capitalise on this.

Numeracy

Don't let your mental arithmetic get rusty. If you have a job in a busy bar taking drinks orders, that should not be a problem. You could also enquire whether your careers service offers the possibility of sitting a practice numeracy test – many do.

Persuasive powers

Can you coax your flatmates into doing their share of the shopping and housework? Do you keep your cool in shops or restaurants when you are not happy with something, yet bring the problem to the notice of the relevant manager? Could you strike a good deal if you were selling something? If not, watch people who are good at this and learn from them.

Problem-solving ability

Part-time jobs, travelling or doing extra-curricular activities can all throw up situations where a problem-solving ability can be useful. It is a good idea to keep a list or log of such instances in case that dreaded question, 'Describe how you have overcome a difficult situation', comes up.

Self-reliance

Most students live away from home and learn to cope. Again, travel outside the UK gives you a head start here. This is a rich source of skills and experience if marketed to employers in a tactical way.

Teamwork

Employers prefer people who participate rather than spend all their time in the library or are interested in sport only as spectators. Build up evidence of membership of sports teams, committees, voluntary work projects, societies or choirs.

Plugging any skills gaps

You can gain some commercial awareness, possibly improve your numerical skills and develop many other skills by undertaking a period of work experience. Don't get to the end of a degree course without it.

Sometimes you will acquire sufficient skills through part-time paid employment. You can learn a lot, even from the most boring work. If you are a shelf filler in a supermarket, for instance, look beyond this relatively humdrum role. Be able to define how your workplace is doing compared with the opposition, its marketing strategies, how it gives customers quality and value, what it could improve, any innovations it has made, how it trains and rewards staff, etc.

There are some excellent formal internship schemes (paid vacation work or graduate experience). Ask your careers service about these, but be aware that competition is at least as tough as it is when going for actual graduate jobs and you will need to apply well in advance – usually the autumn or winter before the vacation in question.

Internships and placements in the 'third sector' (the popular way of referring to charities and not-for-profit organisations) and in the arts and media are usually unpaid. This is not ideal, but it is the way that these sectors operate, so it is a case of biting the bullet and looking at non-salaried opportunities, including volunteering, as an investment in your future. Many of the people in our case studies did this and reaped the rewards. Luke Rosier in Chapter 7 – and others such as Kate Purcell (Chapter 3) – also used routine administration as a passport to higher-level roles in the same sector.

IF AT FIRST YOU DON'T SUCCEED . . .

Several of our case studies had to overcome false starts and barriers to success: Dave Croft and Philip Bassot (Chapters 5 and 13 respectively) left their first courses shortly after starting and Katie Barker (Chapter 12) wasn't always at ease with her choice of higher education. Leaving a degree before completion or obtaining a less than sparkling grade need not hold you back. Recruiters are aware that we live in an imperfect world and make errors of judgement occasionally. These are just minor blips. It's how you deal with them that matters.

BE PATIENT

There's more on job hunting in Chapter 15, but all our case studies provide advice and words of wisdom that should help you. It takes time to find a niche, so don't expect to fall into the job of your dreams straight away. Recent studies by the Institute of Employment Research have shown that:

- The number of graduates entering graduate level jobs has remained steady in the opening years of the 21st century
- About four out of five graduates feel that they are in employment commensurate with their skills
- The vast majority of graduates are working in a job related to their longer-term career plans just three and a half years after leaving university.

Source: The Class of '99: Elias/Purcell/ Davies/Wilton

3 Classics

OVERVIEW

Classics is not widely studied in schools today, but does that make it redundant? There has been a revival of interest in Latin and, to a lesser extent, Greek at secondary level, and those who do undertake these courses report that they have a wider vocabulary (many words in current usage came from these ancient tongues). Even those who quail at the thought of learning such complex languages believe that classical literature in translation is equally useful. '*On a personal level, it's given me a better appreciation of art, for instance,*' says one current undergraduate, '*because so many paintings and sculptures have classical themes. Professionally, that extra insight will be useful if I go into anything involving culture or education.*' Maybe because it has such wide applicability, classics students tend to go into an extremely wide range of careers. The subject equips students to be versatile – probably because, as one of the graduates who features as a case study points out, it covers a variety of disciplines.

WHAT WILL YOU GAIN FROM STUDYING CLASSICS?

Studying for a classics degree helps develop logical thought processes. Not all classics degrees make the study of Latin and Greek mandatory, but both languages are extremely logical, hence many classicists become computer programmers or take up some kind of analytical work. The two languages require care and attention to detail – all those case endings and grammatical agreements.

In addition, you will acquire many of the skills also gained by people who have studied literature or history, depending on the slant of the course and the options you choose. These include communication skills, both oral and written. You will doubtless have to present papers or read reports to a group. You will, in common with all arts students, be expected to research and produce essays.

You will study different societies and cultures, which will encourage flexibility in thinking and you will need to be very disciplined, since you are unlikely to have many lectures each week. In a sense, you will get the best of both worlds: the ability to discuss and reason on topics for which there is no definitive answer plus the ability to provide very precise answers to certain questions where there is a right answer in translation work.

CAREER POSSIBILITIES

Your direct subject knowledge is likely to be of little relevance in a future career unless you decide to teach in higher education, work with a publisher of classical textbooks, go for archive work and museum curatorship or, like one recent graduate, are able to think on your feet and impress an interviewer with your knowledge of retailing derived from studying ancient marketplaces.

A classics degree is well regarded by many graduate employers as it is seen as academically robust, so it is in demand for any career requiring analytical ability – law, the Civil Service, computing and IT, certain careers in finance such as insurance, investment banking and stock market/ financial analysis work, and also for those jobs requiring strong communication skills. Recent raw data taken from two universities shows that in 2008, classicists were working in areas as diverse as fashion buying, TV production, events management and the Army – which just proves how broad their skills base can be!

GRADUATE DESTINATIONS

In 'What do graduates do?', classics is not listed as a separate area but is contained in the statistics for modern languages, and shows that, apart from the 20% who were in clerical and secretarial occupations:

- 14.4% became business and financial professionals and associate professionals (examples given include chartered accountants and business analysts)
- 11.1% became commercial, industrial and public-sector managers (examples given include shipping manager, credit manager)
- 10.5% became marketing sales and advertising professionals (e.g. retail buyer, sales executive).

The remainder fell into a range of other categories; more detailed statistics can be found on the HECSU and HESA websites. (Total number of students surveyed: 3,610.)

The graduates whose case studies we follow have used their skills to enter very different careers.

CASE STUDY

Name: Kate Purcell
Job role: Subject Librarian, Birkbeck College, University of London
Qualifications: *Degrees:* BA Classical Civilisation (First), University of Leeds; MA Library and Information Studies, University College London *A levels:* French, Classical Studies, History, General Studies

Does it seem stereotypical for a classicist to become an academic librarian? Perhaps it does. But Kate is not focusing on her own subject – she's a specialist in Social Sciences and prior to her present job she worked as a librarian in an art college, which is hardly conforming to type. So let's begin at the beginning:

'I went to a traditional girls' grammar school which encouraged pupils towards academic courses. I have to admit that if I'd had more experience of the world, I wouldn't have chosen classics: I would have done something more political such as women's studies or social sciences. Which is what I'm doing now, so it's been a roundabout journey. My course was fairly rigid, mainly literature with some history and philosophy thrown in. I opted for Latin as a subsidiary, but it was possible to take the course entirely in translation.

'I decided to do an ERASMUS placement in Greece, mainly because it was so fantastic to see what I was studying *in situ*, in Athens, but partly because I wanted to travel! It was good fun, although my Greek language skills were not sufficient for me to sit in on lectures. The best thing about the Leeds course was being treated like an adult and being able to do a lot of independent study – though I really only put in the effort doing my final year.'

So what happened after graduation? 'My friends went in all sorts of directions: primary teaching, art conservation, human resources, advertising and marketing, but I didn't really have any idea of what I wanted to do. I took a fairly routine job in banking just to pay the rent and also I figured it was easier to find something more permanent if you were already in employment. I also did a BTEC course in IT because I had no computer skills and I knew I'd need these. As a result, I found work in the University of Wolverhampton as an administrator, helping to research and record graduate destinations. A degree wasn't needed but it was a good starting point.

'I'm interested in politics so I knew that I wanted to work in the public sector – especially after the experience of being in a bank! Like many graduates, I decided to move to London and I found a similar job in the student services department of what is now the University of the Arts. It gave me a lot of freedom to work on specialist projects as well.'

Kate discovered a liking for the information side of the job. She realised that if she wanted to move on, she needed a professional qualification. She moonlighted as a library assistant at the London College of Fashion (LCF) at weekends and for one evening a week, before being accepted on the full-time MA in Library and Information Studies at University College. 'I deliberately chose a traditional course covering historical manuscripts, cataloguing and so on because they were fundamental, whereas other things fall in and out of fashion or can be learned at evening courses. The Master's was intensive, much more of a full-time course than my first degree. By then I knew I wanted to work in the university sector – I enjoyed interacting with students more than with the general public.'

Kate continued to work part time at the LCF while on the MA and returned there after finishing the course, also moving to some of the other art schools connected to the University of the Arts. 'I had a split role at the LCF – part course support and part media librarian. I preferred the former, so when a subject librarian vacancy came up at Birkbeck, I jumped at it. I enjoyed my time at LCF but wanted to work at a so-called traditional university because of the breadth of subject areas, particularly at postgraduate level.'

Anyone who thinks that librarians work in solitary splendour would be surprised by Kate's day-to-day routine. 'I train the students in library skills and do a lot of group work sessions, lectures and one-to-one consultations. I can give support to anyone struggling with their course or with research or hunt down the appropriate resources for postgrads who are covering very specialised areas. It's a bit like being a detective – knowing where to find everything. The main key is understanding where to start sourcing information even if you know nothing about the topic.' Beyond that, Kate's responsibilities at work have grown: 'I'm now in charge of budgets so I'm taking a maths course in order to get to grips with that. And I'm a union rep, so that takes up a lot of my time as well – liaising with staff and management, attending meetings and so forth.'

Skills Kate gained on her degree course . . .

'Independence of thinking and of action – some lecturers wanted you to challenge them which gave me the confidence to question the status quo. That's been useful in many ways!'

. . . and from student life in general

- 'The chance to become involved in student politics.
- My degree is seen as academic and that's useful in a university environment where there is a lot of weight given to the types of subject that you studied. It gives you a certain status.'

Kate's advice

'You need to keep one eye on transferable skills so use your time at university effectively. Unlike sciences, classics doesn't involve 30 hours a week in the classroom, so it gives you plenty of time to manage your work while taking a part-time job, volunteering or joining student societies.'

CASE STUDY

Name: Jake Harders
Job role: Actor
Qualifications: *Degrees:* BA (2.i), MA, MPhil Classics, Trinity College, University of Cambridge; BA Acting (Distinction), Central School of Speech and Drama *A levels:* Latin, Ancient Greek, Ancient History, General Studies

While contributing his case study, Jake was in the middle of rehearsing the Liverpool Playhouse/English Touring Theatre co-production of Roger McGough's translation of Moliere's *The Hypochondriac*. But as you can see from his academic record, his route into the theatre was not straightforward and, in fact, he also went into management consultancy for a while after leaving Cambridge. Jake's motivation for taking a classics degree and going on to study it at an ever higher level was quite straightforward: 'I loved reading Greek drama!' So this perhaps explains the way that his career has progressed and he does feel that his exposure to classics was a help in this process.

'I'd always enjoyed acting and did some plays at Cambridge, but I had no idea how one actually became an actor. I knew that you had to train professionally, and I'd heard of RADA [Royal Academy of Dramatic Art], so I applied there in my final year at university, but was hopelessly unprepared for the rigorous audition process. I learnt a lot from my mistakes, and applied the next year to eight drama schools. I accepted an offer from Central [Central School of Speech and Drama] because it was a free place with a scholarship and I spent three years there training. It's essential to go to one of the top drama schools (RADA, Central, Guildhall, LAMDA [London Academy of Music and Dramatic Art], Drama Centre) in order to get an agent and to develop sufficient awareness of your craft. Central was a place where you could experiment in a relatively safe environment. You could take risks and make mistakes.

Drama school is the gateway to getting an agent. And an agent is the gateway to getting professional, paid work. Both you and your school invite agents to final year plays and showcases. Agents then interview you if they're interested. Sometimes they sign you immediately, or come back to see you in more shows before they make a decision. I was lucky because I had two big roles in my final year, but even without a major part, talented actors will be noticed. One actress had small parts throughout her final year but was so good that she was picked up by a top agent and is now doing amazingly. It's a case of quality not quantity.'

Jake had meetings with several agents before choosing his current representatives, Waring and McKenna. 'Your relationship with your agent is very important – they are connected to the industry, they protect you, advise you, and guide your career in the right direction.' He has been in work pretty much ever since, usually about nine months of every year, in TV, radio and theatre.

'No matter how talented you are, there are several other factors which affect your castability. Your attitude to work, your age, your looks, and also which agent you are with. Some of the top agents like Independent and United Artists have clients at the top of the film industry, others specialise in TV and theatre.' Jake also notes that acting is financially precarious without the ascending career path of most other jobs. 'Only something like 5% of actors work at all. The rest never get a chance. And those who do work often also for quite low wages, unless they work regularly in film and television. So you have to be prepared to live frugally. This may be fine if you're in your twenties with not many financial responsibilities. But if you want to buy a house, get married or start a family, an acting career will require you to think very creatively with your finances.'

When lean periods do come up, Jake needs several other avenues of income. 'Most people need a second job and perhaps a third if you're living just from theatre work. I work in a few box offices. I also do a bit of directing and teaching. Many actors also work in temping jobs, ushering, market research or waiting tables.'

Jake feels that acting is more than just a job – 'it's a calling. It's probably not going to make you rich or successful. But many people do jobs to make money to do things that make them happy. Acting is a strange job which can give you that happiness directly. You could work in an office and be secure, but when I'm on my deathbed I don't want to think "I wish I'd spent more time in front of that computer." '

The skills Jake gained from his degree . . .

- Jake's classics degree gave him no directly useful skills for acting – but he did enjoy it.
- 'From my drama degree I principally learnt good vocal skills – we had an excellent coach called Claudette Williams at Central and

she taught me to control, project, enrich and sustain my voice. She hugely expanded my vocal range.'

■ 'The helpful aspect of a languages degree is constant exposure to text.'

Jake's advice

'Ask yourself why you want to be an actor – if it's anything to do with showing off or becoming a star, you might as well forget it. Those kinds of people tend not to get into drama school. Acting is about collaboration, empathy and compassion, about finding your place in art, not the art in yourself.

Start young enough to have your twenties to see if it works out. And if it doesn't, you're young enough to find a new career. It's a huge leap from being the best actor at school or university to being at drama school where everyone is as good – if not better. And beyond drama school, you have to be strong enough to face constant rejection and competition and disciplined enough to train every day.'

Finally, careers adviser Fiona Thurley, who gives her views in Chapter 15, was a classics graduate too.

4 Creative Arts and Design

OVERVIEW

Creative arts and design covers a huge field. Everything from fine art (painting, sculpture, glass, ceramics, printmaking, to name but a few areas that fall under this title) to 'making' (craft disciplines) and myriad aspects of design (principally two-dimensional, three-dimensional and graphics, and their many offshoots such as theatre, furniture and exhibition design, surface design, packaging, typography . . . the list could go on pretty much for ever). Then there is fashion design and some of its subdivisions such as textiles. And what about illustration, which is often seen to straddle the divide between fine art and graphics? Or conservation (nothing to do with caring for the environment, but focusing on preserving and restoring organic materials and artefacts)? The digital era has also ushered in whole new possibilities for artists, designers and makers to marry new technology with traditional techniques.

WHAT DO YOU GAIN FROM STUDYING CREATIVE ARTS AND DESIGN?

Diverse as they are, all creative arts and design subjects do have some skills in common. Creativity is the obvious link between them and this often goes beyond the ability to make works of art and produce original designs. It can also reveal itself in an ability to think from different angles ('out of the box' as the cliché has it) and come up with new ideas and perspectives. A practical approach, a willingness to accept criticism, imagination and an eye for detail are other common talents that would appeal to employers across the board.

CAREER POSSIBILITIES

At the beginning of their careers, most artists, makers and
designers have to think seriously about how they want to
work. For the first two categories, this could mean setting
up in their own studio; for designers, it might be the decision
between working for just one organisation or taking on
freelance contracts (the latter is not easy when you first
leave art college unless you already have contacts and some
successful commissions behind you.)

For many new graduates there is no choice – they have to
take what's available. Jobs and opportunities are often not
openly advertised, many are obtained through the grapevine
and periods of inactivity can be frequent. Before you start
conjuring up the traditional image of an artist starving in a
garret, take a look at our case studies. It is possible to make a
living from your creative skills and to develop artistically, but
the road can be rocky in places.

At some point, most art and design graduates must decide
whether they want their creativity to support them or whether
they need to take other jobs to support their creativity, i.e. if the
money isn't coming in, what alternative employment will enable
them to keep their artistic endeavours afloat? For this reason,
self-employment and the portfolio style of work mentioned in
Chapter 2 are popular options. Another alternative is to teach
their subject and 'grow' their original work in their free time.
A final possibility is to abandon art as a means of earning a
living. Both our fine art case studies have moved into full-time
roles that don't involve painting. Sarah Walsh is still heavily
involved in the art world, Leah McNally has, as she says, found
alternative ways to express her creativity.

How might more corporate employers view an art or
design degree? One recent graduate made the move from
sculpture to law. Initially it was difficult to market herself
to big solicitors' practices who had never heard of the
prestigious art college that she attended and possibly had
a false impression of what art and design students actually
do. She convinced them by highlighting the skills noted
above and also by pointing out that she had become very

commercially aware through promoting her own work and setting up exhibitions, etc. So making the transition into 'conventional' employment is doable!

GRADUATE DESTINATIONS

The HESA data give an encouraging picture for graduates in this discipline. Unlike many other arts disciplines where a high proportion of respondents went into work unconnected to their studies, a huge number (35.9%) of art and design graduates put themselves in the arts, design, culture and sports professionals category. Two examples of the types of job that came under this heading included graphic artist and photographer on a cruise ship. The more detailed HESA breakdown of the destinations of these graduates shows that:

- 17.4% were working as retail, catering, waiting and bar staff
- 13.5% were in other occupations – a sort of miscellaneous catch-all, which included those in jobs as a chalet host for a ski company and a police officer.

The remainder fell under a range of other headings; more detailed statistics can be found on the HECSU website. (Total number of students surveyed: 8,615.)

CASE STUDY

Name: Sarah Walsh
Job role: Administrator, Whitechapel Gallery
Qualifications: *Degrees:* BA Creative Arts (2.ii), Bath Spa University College; MA Enterprise Management for the Creative Arts, London College of Communication *A levels:* English, Art, Media Studies

Sarah's first degree was a joint course which included both painting and writing. She chose it primarily for the painting, but found that, in part, 'it was a great creative environment' at Bath Spa. The degree included work experience, but what it did not do, at that time, was to provide any tuition or financial pointers in how to set up as an artist. 'There was a gap between university and real life there. I actually didn't understand that career progression was possible. I thought all I could do was become an artist.' So, on graduating, Sarah followed the same route as many creatives before and after her have done: she took casual work, in this case in a deli and bar, to support her art.

'It was a productive time – I took private commissions as well as ones from hotels that required art work and I also collaborated with interior design companies. But after a while it became a struggle and I lost a bit of focus.' At this stage she was also working in a North African inspired store/café and took on a management role there while she got her direction back. It helped her to become aware that she enjoyed public-facing work. For personal reasons, she moved from the Bath/Bristol area to London and found that the streets were not paved with gold. She temped and took administrative roles in a variety of office settings – which ultimately proved useful to her professional development in arts management. 'Getting admin experience was useful. You don't always have to use those skills in a conventional setting: the space that you inhabit can change.'

The real catalyst, however, was Sarah's decision to take a Master's course. 'I came to the conclusion that I would have to do more in order to gain a foothold in the arts world. I chose EMCA [Enterprise Management for the Creative Arts] because it was about enterprise. It gave me the tools to be active and to get back on track. The first thing they asked us to do was a personal audit: what did we want to do and become? That was an enormous help in terms of my career development because unless you know what you are doing and why, you can't learn from it. I think it was only there that I finally realised how to be a student! I was like a sponge. I really wanted to absorb everything.

While on the course, Sarah was looking for an internship and heard about Whitechapel Gallery through a contact. She worked there for free for a while and was delighted to eventually be offered permanent employment there. 'I think my life experience helped in getting me the job, but I also ensured that I made my mark as an intern.' She is a firm believer in the importance of internships, but cautions that you should put in what you want to get out.

Sarah is busy and content in her present post. When I met her she was preoccupied with working through the Arts Council annual submission, not to mention a million other tasks which all contribute to the running of a successful arts venue. But one day the time will come to move on and, perhaps unusually, she thinks that she would like to move somewhere smaller. 'My MA dissertation was on artist-run spaces and I'd like to follow that through at some point. Maybe I'll help to run some studios or a more compact organisation and watch them grow.'

The skills Sarah gained from her degree . . .

- 'I had fun and discovered how to be creative.'
- Knowledge of art.

. . . and from university life in general

People skills.

Sarah's advice

See Chapters 2 and 15 where Sarah looks at arts graduates from an employer's perspective and explains how to approach employers and undertake constructive job hunting.

CASE STUDY

Name: Rachel Liddington
Job role: Brand and Packaging Designer, Vibrandt
Qualifications: *Degree:* BA Graphic Design (2.i), University of Gloucestershire *A levels:* Art and Design, English Literature *Foundation Course*: Theatre Studies

After her A levels, Rachel took two years out and, as she puts it, 'saw a lot of the world'. During her foundation year, she visited the University of Gloucestershire and thought that it had a good feel, not to mention the sort of broad-based course that appealed to her. 'I wasn't sure of which direction I wanted to go, so needed to try a bit of everything. We had just three lectures a week but the studios were open all the time so it was up to you to motivate yourself – not everybody did!'

Rachel particularly appreciated the chance to become involved in external briefs, competitions and activities. The class was encouraged to submit work to major shows and this culminated in a group being invited to 'New Designers' in London, one of the premiere occasions in the design calendar. On top of this, Rachel became year representative for the D&AD Awards and attended this high-profile event.

Rachel found all the staff at the University of Gloucestershire helpful and supportive and she was inspired by one of her tutors in particular. John Brewer arrived at Cheltenham at the start of her third year and he brought a wealth of industrial experience to the degree. 'He made me see what an exciting career this could be. On a practical level, he used his contacts to help us get experience outside the degree. On his recommendation, I went for an interview at my current company, Vibrandt. I worked really hard on my portfolio beforehand! When I got to the meeting, I knew this was exactly right. The people here were cool and exactly what I wanted to be five years down the line.'

Rachel worked unpaid for two and half months, which is standard practice in the design sector: graduates are often formally hired after they have proved themselves in this sort of period. She says, 'It sounds elitist and it's tough financially, but it separates those who really do want it from those who don't. I have friends who are still working for free and I know it's not easy. I thought of it as an investment and dug even deeper into my overdraft.' Her self-belief and hard work paid off and she was taken on permanently.

What does Rachel's job actually entail? 'I arrive at the office at nine and who knows what the day may bring! The account handler may give me a brief to work on for a client: let's say it's packaging for a breakfast cereal, all natural ingredients. I might brainstorm with the client, maybe walk in the park to get some ideas from the surroundings. I'll look for images on the internet and in magazines, then come up with a few rough sketches. They'll go on my wall and, at the end of the day, I'll ask colleagues for comments. I may do a mini spiel about my approach, then, following feedback, I'll filter out what does and doesn't gel.'

Typically Rachel would then collate her best ideas so that she could discuss these with colleagues such as photographers who would contribute to the final designs. She would also send these to the client, who would look at the concept rather than the execution at this stage. Eventually the roughs would go to Vibrandt's Mac visualisers who would work their wizardry before Rachel sends the semi-finished designs back to the client – a process which could be repeated three or four times until everyone is completely happy. 'Once it's perfect, I'm still involved, but other people take over. The artwork stage is very precise and done on cutters. We'll liaise with the printers too to make sure that everything we want is feasible and can be reproduced.'

Months later, Rachel will find the end result on the shelves of her local supermarket. 'It's like watching your babies going out into the world! I get a real buzz when I see people buying "my" products and an even bigger sense of achievement when a client phones to tell me sales are up thanks to my input!'

The skills Rachel gained from her degree . . .

'Apart from graphics skills, the main thing was the ability to make presentations – which I'm still learning. We gave presentations once a month which was quite daunting, but very necessary in this business.'

. . . and from university life in general

'At university, everything is set up to help you achieve anything you want to do. I got motivated and learned to make my own way. This is important because I will have to continue doing this throughout my working life. The competition is intense in this field and if I was laid back I wouldn't last five minutes in my job.'

Rachel's advice

'Say yes to every opportunity and never turn down anything offered to you on a plate. I nearly turned down my original interview with Vibrandt because I felt my portfolio wasn't ready. Use contacts, promote yourself, show passion and energy – it will resonate at interview. I see students coming in now who think it's cool to be arrogant. Be enthusiastic, not aloof, and learn to promote yourself. Finally – never apologise for your work!'

CASE STUDY

Name: Leah McNally
Job role: Director of People and Wildlife, London Wildlife Trust
Qualifications: *Degree:* BA Fine Art (First), Nottingham Trent University *Foundation Course:* Art, Wimbledon School of Art *A levels:* Art, English Literature, Geography

Ever since she was a small girl, Leah had been fascinated by the environment, helping out on the family allotment, joining Greenpeace at a very young age and chivvying her parents to recycle at a time before this was commonplace. Which is perhaps how she ended up in a career that seems a million miles away from exercising her artistic talents.

'My foundation course was very broad and we had a taste of all sorts of creative disciplines, including 3D design, painting, ceramics, graphics, fashion and textiles and theatre design. I decided to specialise in fine art and Nottingham Trent was the ideal place to go. It was a studio-based course and we were all allocated a good proportion of space in which to work – which isn't the case in every art college! I shared my part of the studio with two classmates: it was a good job that they did small-scale work as mine was rather larger and focused around wall-based installations! I was in the studio every day. A whole range of students working in different media used the studios so we had good links with other courses in the building and other contemporary arts students. Again, this is not always the pattern on other visual arts degrees, but it was what I wanted.'

After graduation, Leah was certain in her own mind that she did not want to continue to an MA. She could see little benefit to herself and her practice and also felt that this was just extending her time in one environment. She moved back to London and set up as an artist in her own rented studio. During this period she had six successful exhibitions. But, fairly typically for a creative practitioner, she was also involved in other activities as well.

'I'd had a part-time job on a holiday art play scheme during my university vacations and I continued to do more work for them once I graduated. Then an organisation called Oasis Children's Venture in South London offered me a role in their children's nature garden. Their ethos was nature with a bit of art education mixed in. This reflected the interests I'd had since childhood. I stayed for several years and started doing curriculum-linked environmental sessions for schools and playschemes, some fundraising and a few projects on sustainability. Oasis was involved in the Stockwell Festival and this meshed with my artistic work as well. For three years running, I also worked as a carnival and community artist delivering workshops for children to produce masks and costumes to wear in the parade.' This was a busy period for Leah: she was also undertaking work in a local mental health hospital as part of the Trust Arts Project as an artist working with patients who had mental health problems. As she says, 'I gained experience of working with different client groups that have all ended up being useful in my present role.'

But the time came to move on. She became a community gardener in inner city London with the Bankside Open Spaces Trust (BOST).

'There's not much green space in the area – just small pocket parks really – but I got all sorts of container vegetable schemes up and running, supported by tenants and residents associations, community groups and money from the Neighbourhood Renewal Fund. I set up after school clubs, Saturday family gardening clubs, window box gardening sessions. That covered everyone from 3 to about 85 years old! I used to cycle to children's nurseries with all the stuff in a trailer on the back of my bike, then head on to local old peoples' homes.'

By her second year in post, Leah was managing volunteers and organising schemes for those with mental health issues – which is where her earlier creative endeavours with a similar group came in useful. She counts BOST as a good learning experience, as it had more of a defined and branded image than Oasis and she found out a great deal about how to run a small charity. Still on the search for something different, she then took on two part-time roles as one job. She was both education coordinator for London Wildlife Trust and the coordinator for the London Environmental Education Forum (LEEF).

After a year she moved into her present job, covering education, volunteering, community engagement and youth work, and she now manages a number of nature reserves sites across London, with 18 people working under her and seven reporting directly to her. 'This covers a multitude of people engagement environmental projects. These are all very diverse – we work with faith schools and with adults who have learning difficulties, for instance. We're a partner in the Natural Estates Project, encouraging social housing landlords to "green up" unused land and we've done a pilot on natural play.' As Leah says – no pun intended, I'm sure – 'People and wildlife is definitely a growth area.'

She thinks that if the Oasis job hadn't come up, she may well have stayed with the community arts sector. But in many careers, happenstance can override the best laid plans: she no longer practises as an artist and has given up her studios because, rather than working in isolation as she did back then, she wants to engage with London's communities. However, as she points out, 'I have discovered another outlet for my creativity.'

The skills Leah gained from her degree . . .

Thinking innovatively and creatively – scoping out the whole project, imagining what it will look like on the ground.

... and from university life in general

Being self-motivated and organised. 'Not all of my peers could be seen in the Nottingham Trent studios on a daily basis, but I learned how to manage my workload and the tasks around my artistic assignments. That too has been useful for managing multiple projects as I do now.'

Leah's advice

'Learn and keep learning. Lots of people stay in jobs too long and become deskilled or at least lose opportunities to gain new experiences. I'm fairly unusual in my field because I don't come from an environmental sciences background and have people engagement experience across the board, rather than in one area such as education or youth work. Take advantage of all the free training you get once you are in a job – never say that you don't have enough time!'

5 English

OVERVIEW

All English graduates go into teaching, librarianship, publishing or journalism. Right? Wrong. They are certainly fairly obvious follow-ons from an English degree, and are particularly popular with English graduates, but there would not be enough jobs to go round if every student wanted one of these careers. Many do – and some are disappointed every year. They have to choose alternatives. Other students look into alternatives from the start.

WHAT DO YOU GAIN FROM DOING AN ENGLISH DEGREE?

Like the classicists, you will find little demand for your specialist literary knowledge outside academic and creative employment. However, you should emerge from your degree course equipped to read widely and pick out the information essential to the job in hand, also to argue a case clearly and with conviction.

There are no right and wrong answers where this subject is concerned, so you will learn to weigh up the merits of different arguments and put forward the best (or some of the best) – a useful skill in many managerial jobs or in those involving strategic planning where the best possible or compromise solutions to problems are required.

You will also be an excellent communicator and presenter of material.

CAREER POSSIBILITIES

So English can indeed lead to teaching (including teaching English as a foreign language, which is now a professional career option as well as a temporary role), publishing, librarianship and journalism. It can be extremely useful in advertising and public relations work where creative text has to be produced. Many editors, copywriters, journalists and PR executives have backgrounds in English – but others do not. It is also useful in broadcasting.

This does not mean that English graduates can do only creative jobs. The case studies that follow show graduates working in a range of employment.

GRADUATE DESTINATIONS

'What do graduates do' shows that by far the largest number of English graduates enter administrative work, followed by retail/customer service roles (see below for an explanation as to why this might be the case). Professional roles in education come next. Possibly surprising occupations include air cabin crew and financial advice.

The more detailed HESA breakdown of the destinations of English graduates shows that:

- 19.7% were in clerical and secretarial occupations
- 10% became education professionals (examples given include graduate teacher and teacher of English as a foreign language)
- 9% became commercial, industrial and public-sector managers (examples given include management training with a construction giant and a large insurance company)
- 8.2% became marketing sales and advertising professionals (e.g. market researcher and advertising sales executive)
- 8.2% went into arts, design, culture and sports professions (e.g. news researcher).

(Total number of students surveyed: 4,790.)

CASE STUDY

Name: Beckie Knight
Job role: Widening Participation Development Officer, Royal Veterinary College
Qualifications: *Degree:* BA English Literature and Creative Writing (2.i), Warwick University; MA English Literature, Guelph University, Ontario, Canada *A levels:* English Literature, History, Drama and Theatre Studies

Beckie was the first in her family to go to university and this has impacted on her eventual choice of career, where is she is now actively helping other young people to access higher education and make the most of their potential.

'I did the equivalent of a widening participation scheme while I was in sixth form. It was an additional university application course, very competitive but it helped a great deal in moving me on. I adored university, everything about it, especially meeting a wider variety of people and situations than I could have encountered back in my home town. In terms of my course, I enjoyed the literature side most – I felt there was more to get my teeth into with modules such as Arthurian literature. A lot of people in creative writing were already establishing themselves in that area, so it took me time to connect with this – probably not until my second year.'

Apart from the academic aspects of her life at Warwick, Beckie was extraordinarily busy, holding down a part-time job, becoming a student ambassador, delivering the union paper and popping back home on Saturday mornings to teach drama. She also made the most of her vacations.

'The first summer I was a camp counsellor in Connecticut. It was really the only time I'd been abroad for more than a week, so living in a tent and working with people from all over the world was totally outside my previous experience. The second long vacation I stayed in Warwick with a summer school for gifted and talented young people. I found that experience life changing: I gained more confidence, took on new responsibilities and had creative input into designing activities. I didn't mind the long hours.'

Beckie was such a glutton for punishment that she repeated the process the following year, this time as a senior residential assistant, managing a team. Somehow she also managed to cram in a trip to eastern Europe, having successfully bid for a grant to do an academic project there, collecting folk stories. 'That experience of travelling in a totally unfamiliar society was another important event for me – it made me much more empathetic to different cultures.' It's unclear just how many tales she gathered, but she did come back with a new boyfriend (Dave Croft – see case study below).

During Beckie's final year she took part in a pilot at Warwick for what is now the Student Associate scheme, aimed at tempting undergraduates into becoming teachers. She gained actual teaching experience with Year 7 children and undertook some of the training that the Postgraduate Certificate in Education (PGCE) provides. 'It helped me understand that I didn't want to teach, but I did like being involved in education somehow. I was in the privileged position of having contacts and time to think about where to go next.' This turned out to be Guelph University, Canada. Dave had already mooted the idea of studying for a MA there and the idea of living abroad appealed to Beckie too. Although on the same course as Dave, she took entirely different modules, including a creative writing dissertation and a specialist project on the interaction of the body with technology – all while delivering classes on children's literature to undergraduates: teaching was an integral part of the master's programme.

By now Beckie had decided that she wanted a job in widening participation. Easier said than done: despite her background she lost out for her first few interviews to more experienced candidates and had to work as a house matron in a boarding school to make money. 'Then Lancaster University decided to take a chance on me. I had very little project management and budgeting know-how, but they saw my determination and creativity. I was given the brief of delivering activities in schools in Lancashire and Cumbria and had to run the whole thing – train ambassadors, organise summer schools, write newsletters and reports and design online study groups for gifted and talented pupils and materials for the full range of year groups.'

With all this under her belt, Beckie moved south to join Dave, in a post that had even greater responsibility. 'I'd enjoyed the day-to-day stuff, but wanted a broader remit and the Royal Veterinary College provides this. I still do talks and summer schools, but I also write policy documents, chair the [YG&T] Excellence hub for London and oversee projects. In an odd way it helps that I'm not a scientist. Academic staff run what they've written by me and if I don't understand it they know that it needs re-jigging. I like taking on more and finding out more.'

The skills Beckie gained from her degree . . .

It's evident that she maximised her time at both Warwick and Guelph, but she specifies the following:

- 'teaching skills
- the MA help me to analyse and write in far more depth than my BA.'

. . . and from university life in general

- Organisational ability: 'As an undergraduate there is so little contact time with tutors that you have to get your self sorted.'
- Self-motivation.

Beckie's advice

'Get as much work experience as possible and get your finances sorted out so that you can make full use of every opportunity that presents itself. It's such a short period, but it defines who you will become. Take opportunities and run with them.'

And one final word with her 'widening participation' hat on: 'A lot of students take their time at university for granted. Let people know about university life, so that it filters down to others and inspires them.'

CASE STUDY

Name: Dave Croft
Job role: Graduate Trainee, Civil Service
Qualifications: *Degree:* BA English Language and Literature (First), Leeds University; MA English Literature, Guelph University, Ontario, Canada *A levels:* English Literature, History, Government and Politics

Prior to joining Leeds, Dave had a false start at another university where he had taken English and American Studies, mainly seduced by the promise of studying in the USA. He left the course and spent the rest of the year working in a garden centre and doing placements on two local papers.

'Leeds was fantastic, a much better choice for me. The core content took me through the whole literary canon from medieval to contemporary and there was an equally diverse set of optional subjects. We worked in small seminar groups and the teaching was good. Looking back, if I was applying again, I would have taken English and politics – just because the knowledge base would have been so useful – but, at the time, I was more than content.'

Once he had completed his degree, Dave decided to extend his education by taking an MA in Canada. 'I wanted to look beyond the UK, but I also needed somewhere where they spoke English. Canadian fees were not as hefty as those at home and there was the bonus of being able to teach on some undergraduate courses, which was great – it gave me all sorts of transferable skills. The master's as a whole was quite stressful in places – but it certainly developed my analytical skills to a much greater extent than my time as an undergraduate.'

Dave enjoyed the research too, although, again, with hindsight he would have focused on something along the lines of international relations, policy or security. He flirted with the idea of going into academia but then, as he puts it, 'came to my senses'. His stint with the local press had persuaded him against journalism and from then on he had always known that he wanted to go into the Civil Service. While in Leeds, he got a summer internship at a government department between his second and third years. As part of a communications section, this entailed a fair amount of responsibility – editing an internal newsletter, writing a paper about the objectives of the intranet and liaising with other regions about database use.

'I applied for the Civil Service Fast Stream, but only got through two of the three selection stages. So I took a couple of temporary jobs, one in the private sector and the other in the tribunal service, which is effectively a civil service department: I think this did help later on.' Dave then saw an advertisement for a paid internship at the Home Office. It was another challenging application process, but this time he made it and spent seven months at the Ministry of Justice, working on a range of assignments in what was essentially a development role. He took part in high-level meetings, helped with budget setting and looked at approaches to risk management. As part of this he met Fast Streamers already in post and speaking to them was a good preparation for the competency-based interviews that the Civil Service favours. Maybe that was why when he applied for two jobs he was successful in both.

'I'm now in my second posting with the Fast Stream. It's a policy role based around dealing with serious crimes. I attend ministerial meetings and write briefings for "my" ministers. I'm also liaising with stakeholders, police, academics and other government departments in coming up with ideas and strategies.'

The skills Dave gained from his degree . . .

- 'Using analytical skills to present clear cogent arguments.
- Assessing qualitative data.
- Writing, oral presentations and the full range of research skill.
- Learning to read quickly.'

But Dave also points out what he didn't learn and what would be useful to him now. 'Hitting really tight deadlines: you may think that you do that at university, but there is usually some leeway. That doesn't exist at work!'

. . . and from university life in general

'I made great friends and it broadened my horizons.'

Dave's advice

'It may sound as if I was very focused but I went through phases of uncertainty about my future, the same as most people. I think it's important to go about creating opportunities for yourself. Definitely apply for jobs and internships. Even if you are unlucky this will be the source of other possibilities, so make sure that you talk to people and put yourself "out there".'

6 Film and Media Studies

OVERVIEW

When we talk about media, what do we actually mean?
A strict dictionary definition would be 'a means of
communication'. When media studies first emerged as a
degree subject, it often fell into two distinct categories: the
written message (publishing, advertising, journalism) and
the visual/aural message (film and broadcasting). At that
stage the internet had not been invented and the digital
revolution was just a gleam in someone's eye. The term now
has a wider connotation and traditional media have often
been absorbed by new technology or run parallel with it, e.g.
we now have e-books and online newspapers as well as the
printed equivalent, marketing and advertising is often done
electronically and via hard copy, and sound, images and
technology come together through multimedia applications.
The case studies in this chapter show the wide choice of
media courses – and associated jobs – that are now available.

WHAT WILL YOU GAIN FROM STUDYING FILM AND MEDIA SUBJECTS?

There's hot debate about whether film and media degrees
actually equip people to work in those sectors. If we are
talking about film and TV, how telling is it that if you want
to read case studies from this area you won't find them here,
but rather in Chapter 7 (History) and Chapter 12 (Performing
Arts)? Certainly talented graduates from every possible
degree discipline can and do make it in the media. Does this
mean that a film and media qualification is not worthwhile?
There is some perception out there that the subject just
involves watching films and messing about in studios for
three years. This may be unfair! Plenty of media graduates do

get jobs in TV and film, but, like everyone else, they have to get out into the 'real world' and learn about the sector from the bottom up – usually as runners.

A university course, however good, is rarely seen as a substitute for actual work experience. This is true in all branches of the media industry: would-be journalists are expected to have served their time on a magazine or newspaper, whether or not they possess a 'relevant' degree. Ditto advertising, as Charlotte Driscoll's case study proves here (and Philip Bassot's in Chapter 13). Jamie MacCarthy, the first profile that you will read in this chapter, tells us how much he has learned in his various jobs, from classmates and through extra-curricular activities, as well as from his first degree.

However, David Wheeler of 'Start in TV' website thinks a degree course can provide good experience. *'It is simply an academic degree and sometimes it is perceived as not rigorous enough for the purpose, but that can vary from university to university. Some courses have got a very good reputation.'* David teaches on the BA Media Production course at Staffordshire University and cites this as a good example of a practical course that prepares students for life on the set, in the studio, the editing suite or the cutting room. *'They have to make 10 films in three years, so that's pretty intensive.'*

So if you do decide to take a film or media degree (whether undergraduate or postgraduate), check what it contains and how it is structured (see the Course Finder on www.ucas.com). 'Media studies' can mean different things to different people and content varies widely. The best courses will give you an overview of all the areas that make up this complex profession. You need to be constantly aware of changes going on in all aspects of the industry and be open to new ways of working and the possibilities of channelling different resources (together or separately) to get your message across.

CAREER POSSIBILITIES

David goes on to say that in film and programme making, an essential skill is story telling: what you are producing, whether it's factual or fictional, needs to have a beginning, a middle and an end, with strong characters, a goal in sight and some conflict that threatens the outcome. Look for a course that enables you to master this, whatever your specific area of interest. He also points out that a good journalistic instinct – a nose for a story – is needed in film and TV and that the best producers often come from this side of 'media' (whether via formal study, student experience or on-the-job training).

So the truth may be that film and media studies is a useful foundation and, at its best, can provide valuable skills that are applicable across the whole sweep of graduate jobs. Courses that teach both creative thinking and practical techniques, that harness students' imagination and ideas and that provide technical know-how have obvious benefits in any job market. But they may be a starting point rather than an end result.

GRADUATE DESTINATIONS

From the HESA data for film and media graduates, an interesting picture emerges which redresses the balance a little. Unlike many other arts disciplines where a high proportion of graduates went into administrative work, followed by retail/customer service roles, many media studies graduates confirmed that they had jobs in the arts, design, culture and sports professionals category – which is the one most appropriate to their education. Admittedly, this tied with the retail and catering group, with clerical and secretarial occupations coming a close third, but it compares very favourably to, for instance, the overall findings for English and history. Marketing, sales and advertising professionals scored strongly as a destination area too. The HESA data showed:

- 17.5% became arts, design, culture and sports professionals (examples given include camera operator/video editor, media assistant in online games)
- 17.5% were working as retail, catering, waiting and bar staff, with 16.2% working in other clerical and secretarial occupations

- 13.6% specified other (e.g. visual merchandising assistant, call centre operator)
- 10.1% were marketing, sales and advertising professionals (e.g. trainee account executive in a media agency)
- 10.1% became commercial, industrial and public-sector managers (examples given include management training with a construction giant and a large insurance company).

(Total number of students surveyed: 2,955.)

CASE STUDY

Name: Jamie MacCarthy
Job role: Web Advertisement Designer, www.jobs.ac.uk, and portfolio worker in sound, media and web design
Qualifications: *Degrees:* BSc in Music, Technology and Innovation (2.i), De Montfort University; currently taking a part-time MA in Media Arts at Coventry University *BTEC National:* Music Technology *GNVQ:* Media Studies *A level:* English (not completed)

Illness forced Jamie to leave his GNVQ course. When he returned to college again he took a BTEC with no real thought of continuing to university. At the time he was very busy beyond his studies, playing in bands, doing some music promotion, writing about the local rock scene and 'messing around with computers'.

'A tutor pointed out that I could go on to university, so I did some research and ended up at De Montfort. I would say there was a high drop out rate to begin with because it wasn't what people expected, but it gradually all came together, especially in the third year. We did do some theory and academic assignments looking at broader cultural issues, but basically it was very practical. My focus was in sound and music for interactive media such as video games and web applications. A lot of employers such as established producers and directors came in to talk to us and lead tasks. We also collaborated with other courses – film studies for example. I was one of only two people with an interest in sound, so I would help out with Foley (a specialised tool used in sound production), other effects and post-production techniques.'

When Jamie graduated, he became involved with all kinds of contract work relating to his subject and his interests. One of his main roles is with the leading academic recruitment site www.jobs. ac.uk, affiliated to Warwick University.

'I design web-based adverts, sometimes for single jobs, often for entire recruitment campaigns. I like making and manipulating websites and I do other freelance web design assignments, along with podcasts and internet radio projects. A lot of it is very much DIY: you get to know one program and then you can gradually pick up others such as Flash as you go along. I play around with various types of software and hardware at work and at home. Once I have an inkling of how they function, I can teach myself by using the transferable technical skills from my degrees and my various jobs. For instance, I mastered Max MSP (a package for creating virtual musical instruments) as a result of what I learned at De Montfort. In any computer-related discipline, people swap ideas and tips, but you constantly need to keep up to date with emerging technology.'

Jamie remains very enthusiastic about working with sound and has a home studio, but is now also engaging with the visual side of digital and multimedia applications. He knew someone taking MA Media Arts at Coventry and was enthused about its potential. 'It's much more about the use of visuals and many of the other students are illustrators and designers, so this is giving me a whole new outlook and a complementary set of skills. I've helped with interactive installations and can now use video cameras and programs such as ActionScript. One bonus is that, at De Montfort, we are able to access and experiment with equipment that would be out of our reach if we wanted to buy it ourselves. The course is linked to the local centre for creative enterprise, which promotes the innovative possibilities of art in new media contexts for graduates of all creative disciplines.'

Jamie reckons that this eclectic background helps to keep his work fresh and exciting. 'If I'd taken a very specific degree – say web design – I might not now be so into that now, because it would have become routine. Because I'm doing so many different things, everything merges and interlinks.'

The skills Jamie gained from his degree . . .

- Dealing with technical problems in different media environments.
- Being able to explain obscure technology to people who don't understand it, to help them realise what can and can't work.
- 'Because I've got technical know how, I can be more inventive and resourceful at work and I can also put more time into planning ahead, meeting deadlines and managing projects, which are things you can't really grasp at university.'

… and from university life in general

Jamie is glad that he took his first degree slightly later than is usual. His experience of life and of music/sound helped him take a more balanced view of his course and to combine it with his extra-curricular activities – he carried on playing music for instance. The first degree and now his MA have helped him to explore and discover different sides to what he wanted to do.

Jamie's advice

'Degrees and master's courses aren't for everyone and you may not even need it if you want to perform, to make films, to create. It's easy to get so caught up in your subject that you burn yourself out. People aren't necessarily ready for university straight out of sixth form or even after a gap year, so take things at your own pace. This line of work and the freelance lifestyle aren't for everyone. It can be tough making a living, but it suits me well and has brought me all sorts of extra interests and outlooks.'

CASE STUDY

Name: Charlotte Driscoll
Job role: Account Manager, Mason Zimbler (creative digital marketing agency)
Qualifications: *Degree:* BA Advertising (First), University of Gloucestershire *Foundation Course:* Art *A levels:* Art, English, Biology, Chemistry

Unsure whether to pursue arts or sciences, Charlotte hedged her bets with her A levels, but eventually decided that she liked the arts more. After attending an open day at the University of Gloucestershire in Cheltenham, she felt in tune with the atmosphere there. The campus and the town were big enough to do lots of things that she enjoyed, but sufficiently small scale to get around easily. Her foundation art course had included graphics, but she knew that she didn't want to focus on that, so she chose the degree because it was a mixture of art and copywriting.

'It was one of the few practical advertising courses in the country and, having had a placement in an agency at GCSE level, I thought I might like to specialise in this. It was all creative: the theory was pretty relaxed and there was no real business input. Looking back now, I think that this was something they could usefully add.'

In the advertising world, copywriters work closely with designers and often apply for jobs together, so the degree paired up students and gave each of them the chance to try both roles on alternating assignments. There was a certain amount of 'changing partners' in the early part of the course, but Charlotte eventually teamed up on a more permanent basis with one member of her class. They worked so well together that they won a placement with a well-regarded advertising agency.

'We were disappointed that it didn't culminate in a job offer. They asked us to do more placements and come back in a year.' This wasn't feasible financially because by now Charlotte had graduated and needed paid employment. Her partner eventually decided to return to her home town, while Charlotte persevered alone, going to about 20 interviews over a six-month period. 'It was very frustrating: I thought that because I had a First that might make a difference, but it just didn't happen.' But all's well that ends well. Charlotte finally landed an account handling job at Mason Zimbler, a technology-based agency with an impressive list of corporate clients.

'My course wasn't particularly relevant, as you can do this with pretty much any degree. It's not a creative position. I act as the interface between the creatives and the client.' This means managing the day-to-day jobs that contribute to each client account: taking initial briefs from the client; writing specific briefs for the different colleagues involved such as copywriters and designers; progress chasing, monitoring and reviewing the finished work; booking the work out and delivering it to its final destination; then following through to make sure that the client is happy and satisfied. If that sounds hectic, bear in mind that Charlotte picked up the individual components of the work as she went along.

'The work is IT specific so I've had to get my head round all the terminology and technology, not to mention the business and finance aspects. I even had to learn how to use a PC! I was used to working on a Mac. I was thrown in at the deep end and I managed to swim!'

The skills Charlotte gained from her degree . . .

■ 'Presentation skills. We had no formal training in this, but we learned through doing it. You find out what to do and what not to do by watching other people. Practice made perfect.'

- The confidence that came from carrying out assignments and presentations successfully.

… *and from university life in general*

'It really depends on what you put into it. Choose the right place and course!'

Charlotte's advice

'When you're looking for jobs, do your background research. In the advertising and marketing world it's important to have good organisational skills, to understand customer service and to show some sound common sense.'

CASE STUDY

Name: Stacey McIntosh
Job role: Journalist, editor, and currently Communications Assistant, University of London External System distance learning programme
Qualifications: *Degree:* BA Multimedia Journalism (2.i), Bournemouth University *A levels:* Art and Design, English Literature, Media Studies

'I chose Bournemouth because it had an outstanding reputation as teaching one of the best undergraduate degrees in journalism. What was especially good about it was the 50/50 mix of practical and academic. One day you could be filming or making a programme, the next you might be studying shorthand or learning about media law. The course looked at all forms of journalism – broadcast (TV, radio) and print (newspapers and magazines). They've now added a module about online content too.'

Stacey feels that the degree really did try to prepare people for life in journalism and for professional exams and placed particular emphasis on work experience. 'We took the National Council for the Training of Journalists (NCTJ) qualification, which is something of an industry gold standard and tremendously useful on a CV. I'd highly recommend it. In addition, we were encouraged to do at least a fortnight's placement in our first year and double that in year two.' Stacey exceeded that bare minimum, finding all kinds of opportunities in TV, radio, papers and periodicals. He stresses that it was an excellent way to make contacts.

On leaving Bournemouth, Stacey initially worked on a short-term contract, putting together a global events diary which could be used by subscribers in the media industry and then he moved on to another transitory role as a press office assistant and communications forward planner with another agency. Like many graduates before him, he found that a vocational degree does not automatically lead to work. 'Journalism is hugely competitive and it took me quite a while to get started.' His opportunity came when he found another temporary post for an assistant editor at Hobsons, which produces magazines and web materials about careers and education.

'I ended up staying for over two years and was promoted to an editor's role, working on publications for international students. I did some writing but the rest of my work included planning content, commissioning writers, page layout, subediting and proofreading. I created publications for external clients as well.' It was a busy time, but Stacey and several colleagues were eventually made redundant in a cost-cutting exercise.

After two months seeking work, a friend told Stacey about opportunities on London's free *Metro* newspaper. He contributed to their website on and off for a year, writing news stories and items on entertainment and the arts. When a vacancy for a features subeditor came up, he was taken on permanently – the team was glad to take a known quantity on board. The job covered layout, plus the writing of film and restaurant reviews and some sport and cultural features. Then – redundancy again. 'I think the industry accepts that this is an occupational hazard, and we all realise that we'll have to move around, rather than stay with one company.'

Stacey's new job as communications assistant is different again: much of it will be writing newsletters and press releases about the university's distance learning department's new IT systems, which go live by 2012. Stacey was just getting to grips with it when he contributed this case study: his career journey so far shows how broad a career in media can be.

The skills Stacey gained from his degree . . .

- 'All the technical skills came in handy. I still use shorthand and it's a good thing to have when your digital recorder breaks down in the middle of an interview! Media law came into its own when I was

editing at *Metro*. If I did need to film – say to put something onto a website – I still could, so it's a bit of a selling point.'
- 'The news writing part of the course was excellent: we had to produce coherent articles of 250 words in 10 minutes – great for teaching you to meet deadlines and be organised.'

. . . and from university life in general

'I made good friends on the course and, now, a few years down the line, they've also turned into contacts who might be able to help my career in future. It's probably not something that I'd have thought about when I graduated at 21, but keeping up those links is really important.'

Stacey's advice

'As above – make the most of your contacts! Also try and get a range of work experience with big and small companies so that you see both sides of the industry. If I was starting out again, once I'd found my niche, I'd try to keep returning to the same placement, so that I got my face known and would be hopefully offered permanent work. This happened to a friend of mine who was taken on by a music magazine for whom he'd done several placements and is still there! But this job isn't necessarily about going out and meeting celebrities: a lot of it is desk work and phone interviews and getting particular messages across – not all of them objective. There are many positives too, of course, but you need luck as well as talent and hard work.'

7 History

OVERVIEW

History graduates have some fairly obvious careers to consider, namely teacher, archivist, museum curator and librarian. These make direct use of the subject. But dozens choose alternative careers, many of which are totally unrelated to history – as shown by our three case studies.

WHAT SKILLS WILL YOU GAIN FROM STUDYING HISTORY?

Researching, understanding and analysing issues are major ones. You will also learn to put forward ideas and arguments clearly, while the ability to read widely, deal with vast amounts of information and pick out what is relevant are skills familiar to all historians. Students frequently refer to the sheer mass of material they must sift through in order to write just one essay.

You will be able to organise facts logically and to condense material and write concisely – a very useful ability in many jobs that call for the preparation of written reports or the giving of oral briefings or presentations. The range and breadth of job possibilities for historians is almost infinite but you can get some indication of the scope by looking at the data below. It seems that, with history, anything is possible!

CAREER POSSIBILITIES

Careers that make use of these skills very heavily include law, journalism, local government administration and high-level work in the Civil Service – helping to formulate policy and advising ministers. You could consider anything from making sales pitches in an advertising agency to preparing reports on a potential company for takeover in investment banking.

GRADUATE DESTINATIONS

The detailed HECSU breakdown of the destinations of history graduates shows that:

- 20.8% were in clerical and secretarial occupations
- 13.8% were in retail, catering and bar work
- 14% went into occupations defined as 'other', such as a volunteer coordinator with the Red Cross (see Luke Rosier's case study in this chapter)
- 11.1% were commercial, industrial and public-sector managers (examples given include trainee retail manager and a development manager with the Home Farm Trust)
- 10.6% were business and financial professionals and associate professionals (e.g. HR management and stockbroking).

The remainder fell into a range of other categories. More detailed statistics can be found at www.hecsu.ac.uk. (Total number of students surveyed: 4,515.)

CASE STUDY

Name: Jess Brammar
Job role: Assistant Producer, Current Affairs, Mentorn TV
Qualifications: *Degree:* BA International History and Russian (First), London School of Economics *A levels:* History, English Literature, Theatre Studies

'I really didn't intend to go to university at all. As soon as I left school, I went to work in financial services. So when I did make up my mind that I wanted to study, I was absolutely committed.

The LSE [London School of Economics] course was one that you could put together as you liked: it was very flexible, which is how I came to take up Russian. The history element concentrated on modern times, especially the Third World and international politics. It was brilliant for any job in current affairs and many graduates of my year went into those sorts of roles. It gave us a kind of manual for all of the conflicts in today's world. And I think I learned just as much from my fellow students as I did from the actual degree content: looking at issues in the Middle East from the perspective of both Israeli and Palestinian classmates was an eye opener. It couldn't have been a better grounding for what I do now.'

How did Jess get into TV, a highly competitive field? 'I always knew I wanted to be a journalist, but if someone had mentioned TV to me I would have been horrified. I really wasn't into entertainment at all. I did bits and pieces of work experience throughout my time at LSE and contributed to a student magazine. I interned at the *New Statesman* and found a placement at the BBC World Service (Russian section) by sending an email to them. A bit cheeky but it worked!'

Jess also used her persuasive powers to obtain a spell of work on the *Today* programme last summer as a sort of secondment while *Question Time* was off the air.

'I ended up at Mentorn because a contact, who is now my present boss, was interested in bringing on young people who wanted to go into TV. He gave me a half hour interview and, when he moved to *Question Time*, offered me some (poorly!) paid experience. This led to short-term contracts as a researcher, which gradually turned into something more permanent. I had planned to go on to a postgraduate course to learn more about editing and that aspect of production, but this opportunity came up first.'

On a daily basis, what does Jess do? 'We're a small team – just one editor, one producer and two assistant producers. I share the role of booking panellists for the programme and now have good professional relationships with many of our regulars. I also have to take note of key themes and issues and use these to write notes for the presenter – suggesting questions, lines of attack and so on. Two days per week we are out on location filming: *Question Time* goes out live on a Thursday night and then is cut to half an hour for a repeat on Friday. I do get involved with the technical side though I have no formal training in that. It's just something you are expected to do and you pick it up on the job. The first couple of times I did it, it was nervewracking and frightening but there is always a technical colleague around to help.'

Jess sees definite prospects ahead for herself: 'Because Mentorn is a small company, I should be able to progress, unlike some of the bigger broadcasting organisations where it takes longer to move forward. I'll probably earn less than some of my former classmates but I just love the job.'

The skills Jess gained from her degree . . .

All the skills that she is using now:

- distilling information: looking at the wider picture, then refining and condensing it
- research: 'I started out as a researcher and this still forms part of my duties'
- the ability to be discerning about sources of information – some are more reliable than others.

. . . and from university life in general

- Being part of the student magazine was invaluable – most of that team have now gone into some form of journalism.
- Broader world knowledge – not just of history and current affairs, but from visiting Russia in the summer breaks. Jess was lucky enough to get a bursary for this part of her studies and spent time in St Petersburg before adventurously travelling to Siberia by train.

Jess's advice

'If you want to get into TV, make sure you get loads of work experience and maximise this on your CV: it shows that you really want it. If you don't do that, there will be plenty of others ready to step in ahead of you. It's unfortunate that placements tend to be unpaid, but that's the way it works. And when you are starting out, be prepared to do things that aren't in your job description – there are often changes at the last minute and you'll be expected to muck in.'

CASE STUDY

Name: Luke Rosier
Job role: Project Supervisor, Voluntary Service Overseas
Qualifications: *Degrees:* BA History (2.i), Royal Holloway, University of London; MA Modern History, University College London *A levels:* History, English, Sociology

Luke found his degree flexible in that it linked social and cultural history and he could adapt it to his own interests. 'I love novels and paintings and found that the course allowed me to look at them in their historical context. I could then go on to make a connection between what was taking place then in art and literature and what is happening now. It was also possible in theory, at least, to take modules at other colleges of London University, but in my case, timetable clashes prevented this!'

Having taken a gap year after A levels, Luke was initially slow to get back into the swing of study. 'It took me a term or two to find my feet. I just muddled through for the first year, coasted along in the second and it was only during the third year that I really hit my stride. I decided to do an MA because I wasn't finished with studying yet and also because I was contemplating a career as an academic. I rationalised this by telling myself that if I did go into academia, a master's would be a prerequisite, and, if I decided not to pursue that particular option, a second degree wouldn't be a bad qualification to have.'

Despite his obvious enthusiasm for the subject, Luke at first underestimated the amount of commitment needed for an MA. 'I started off as a full-time student, but I was also working as well and this didn't allow me to give my studies the attention which they deserved. In the end, I switched to the part-time master's over two years which allowed me to combine the course with a job. I benefited from having some excellent tutors and the space to explore ideas, while honing my writing and research skills.'

Luke eventually decided against becoming an academic, and, like many graduates in this situation, found the hunt for work an uphill struggle. He was interested in getting into the highly popular heritage or arts management sectors: 'When you're studying you can more or less indulge yourself, but when you're looking for your first job, you're up against some very talented people – often for very basic roles.'

He took some work experience in a gallery before deciding that a role in the visual arts was not for him. After another two or three months with little success in finding a niche, he decided that he just needed to take any suitable job in order to get started. This turned out to be a short-term paid position as a receptionist at Voluntary Service Overseas [VSO], a well-established major charity specialising in international aid and development. 'I suppose I was uncertain about it at first. I was interested in the field, but hadn't considered it as a possible career.' Despite this apparently unpromising beginning, the job 'ignited a passion I hadn't felt in any of my previous work experience. It gave me the chance to look at the charities and NGOs from a different, professional, perspective. I could see that it valued people, that it delivered on a global scale and I decided that I could justify spending another year trying to establish myself in this area. Being a receptionist was brilliant for this as I got to know everyone

What Can I Do With ... an Arts Degree?

in the organisation – cleaners, CEO and anyone in between – and they knew me. I found out about the structure of VSO and similar setups and really got to grips with the sector.'

VSO offered Luke another three-month contract and then, through a mixture of what he defines as 'perseverance and developing my job application skills', he was taken on as a programme administrator in its International Programmes Group. He spent 18 months there 'cementing my skills', before having a first taste of travelling abroad, in this case to the tiny ex-Soviet republic of Tajikistan. With all this experience under his belt, Luke was ready to take on his next challenge as VSO's programme supervisor for volunteering. This involved going up to Edinburgh by himself to sort out community placements and accommodation for volunteers in the city. He also arranged publicity and put everything in place for the arrival of nine UK and nine Chinese volunteers, plus Luke's counterpart in China. Once that was up and running, he moved to China for a few months to oversee the second phase of the project there.

What comes next? Yet more exotic places! 'I'm working with the British Council on behalf of VSO and we are forging links between volunteers in Brighton and Bahrain.' It will mean Luke upping sticks yet again and moving to the south coast, but he relishes the prospect of gaining further experience in a different community. 'When I took on Edinburgh, which was a fixed contract, I had to make a conscious decision to move from a permanent job to a series of short-term assignments. Working in this way isn't for everyone – it would be difficult if you had family responsibilities for instance – but it suits me.'

The skills Luke gained from his degree . . .

- The knack of reading and writing clearly and drawing on this to present ideas coherently. 'This is important if you're writing a report and outlining a country profile for the website or if you're bidding for funding.'
- Speaking in seminars meant learning how to articulate ideas carefully and this is another strength that Luke has taken to VSO.
- 'Research, of course, which has come in very useful now – when I'm investigating the feasibility of working in a new country, for instance.'
- Taking and analysing an argument and also putting forward an argument in a positive and objective way.

. . . and from university life in general

- Independent living.
- Finding out what interests you in the world.
- Watching friends' progress – seeing what different things they do and how their careers develop.

Luke's advice

'If you want to work for an NGO, it's highly competitive. Even if you've studied a "relevant" discipline such as international development, you'll still need to do an internship or some volunteering. If you can't find this sort of placement in an NGO then look at local community organisations. Don't be too fussy: lots of volunteers and interns are eventually given paid positions. Don't be put off by rejections, but learn from them: if you persist, someone will see your worth.'

CASE STUDY

Name: Claire Simmonds
Job role: Intern (Mountbatten Institute Internship Programme), hedge fund company, New York
Qualifications: *Degree:* BA History (2.i), University of Leeds *A levels:* History, English, Sociology

'The history course at Leeds was very broad in the first year and ranged from medieval to modern. It was a good overview but no real chance to get your teeth into anything. From Year 2 onwards there was an amazing array of modules – for instance I took electives on both Ancient Greece and 20th Century Politics. In the final year, I concentrated on Ancient Greece and, for my dissertation, I undertook original research into the influence of Sparta on Hitler and the Third Reich. Very little had been written about that so it really tested my investigative skills.'

When Claire graduated, she used family contacts to secure a temporary administrative contract at Imperial College, covering for someone on maternity leave. She found it offered excellent experience – and good pay! But she was already looking beyond London and across the Atlantic. 'I'd been to New York twice and I knew that I wanted to spend more time there. I'd found about Mountbatten in my final year, merely by googling "New York + internships", so, while I was at Imperial, I was busy with the selection process for the scheme. The system is that you pay a small fee then they sort out accommodation, salary and an appropriate placement for successful candidates. It's almost like "Where's the catch?" '

Well, of course, there was a catch – a series of interviews – but Claire sailed through these with aplomb. She found that the first interview 'was about you as a person. They boast that they take the cream of graduates in their early 20s from the UK and all over the world too, but it's no good just being intellectually outstanding. They're not interested in your academic record beyond the set educational requirements. They wanted to know how you'd cope with living abroad, what you had to offer to the Mountbatten Programme, they explored your interests and basically they were looking for well-rounded people.'

Once Claire had been accepted, her profile was sent to the Mountbatten office in New York, and forwarded to relevant employers whenever an appropriate opportunity came up. It wasn't cut and dried: she had to go through more interviews and was always in competition with other would-be interns. 'Sometimes you received a reasonable amount of notice before your phone interview and other times it could be just a couple of hours. I had the interview for this job at 8pm one evening, with just one hour to prepare for it and learned that they'd decided to take me on by 10pm. As that was just about 10 days before I was due to fly to the States, it was a bit nerve wracking. Other people knew where they were going months ahead, but it was just the luck of the draw.'

Claire now shares an apartment with other Mountbatten interns in New Jersey and crosses the Hudson River every day to go to work in a classic brownstone building, rather than a skyscraper office block. The small hedge fund company for which she works was set up by two executives who disliked the corporate environment. Her actual job title is research administrative assistant. 'We are event driven and we look for companies that aren't doing so well, which is where I come in. I have to check what's happening using reports such as those issued by Reuters and I also use the internet to obtain factual information. It can be pretty full on.'

Claire had no thoughts of working in finance originally – she just wanted to be in the Big Apple. But now she sees the positive benefits of choosing this role, especially now that, when she returns to the UK, she has decided to try to make the move into publishing. 'I do feel that a background in finance is invaluable whatever you go on to do and the beauty of working for this particular organisation is that we're so compact. I can see what everyone else does and get involved in that to some extent. It's given me an understanding of other areas such as marketing.'

The skills Claire gained from her degree . . .

- 'Research of course – that's so true even though it is a bit of a cliché.'
- The ability to separate good facts and information from those that are less reliable. She feels that she can now sift through numerous books and resources and quickly gauge what will be useful and what can be discarded.

. . . and from university life in general

Leeds offered Claire the chance to make good friends from all sorts of backgrounds: she describes it as a real melting pot. She has also stayed in touch with many of her tutors. She found that, by being part of such an eclectic group, she broadened her knowledge of different subjects and learned about what other people were studying and experiencing.

Claire's advice

'If you intend to do a history degree, make sure that it offers what you want. Not every university provides such a wide curriculum and choice of modules as Leeds does. My feeling is that modern history is really just politics, which is fine if that's what you want, but I loved the fact that I was able to focus on Ancient Greece.

At university and beyond, put yourself forward for everything. For me, it was pretty daunting to apply to Mountbatten and to aim at going to New York. I knew that my chances of getting in weren't that high. But I went for it – and so should you!'

CAREER NOTE

The Mountbatten Institute was set up to foster international and cross-cultural understanding among young people from across the world and to provide opportunities for development and personal growth. Each year it offers a limited number of paid internships in New York and London, mainly to graduates, and also for a few candidates with A levels or equivalent.

8 History of Art

OVERVIEW

It's a myth that history of art is a vocational course. Not all graduates go into picture restoration (wrong – that is a career that requires specialist practical and technical skills), fine art valuation, antique dealing or art gallery management. There simply are not enough jobs in these fields to go around and 'relevant' jobs are hugely competitive. Find out more about alternatives by looking at our two very diverse case studies.

WHAT WILL YOU GAIN FROM STUDYING HISTORY OF ART?

By studying this subject you'll obtain almost identical skills to those gained on a general history course (see Chapter 7) – and more! The late Welsh art historian Clare Rendell once explained how art historians had an edge on other graduates. She maintained that their education gave them the chance to get under the surface and go beyond the obvious in their thinking, making them ideal for careers where it is necessary to consider issues from different angles and to come up with new perspectives. Clare also pointed out that art history itself is riddled with all kinds of social, political and economic influences and classical allusions, giving graduates a wide general knowledge and breadth of understanding.

CAREER POSSIBILITIES

Some graduates do enter the careers mentioned above. These are the directly vocational possibilities, as are art critic (a very small field), museum curator (usually following a specialised MA) and inspector of historic buildings. Most openings for this work – and there are not many – are with the national heritage organisations. Other occupations, in which the degree is particularly relevant, include heritage management, picture research, librarianship and publishing.

GRADUATE DESTINATIONS

'What do graduates do?' does not cover art history but it is usual for graduates to go into all kinds of careers, from book production, publishing and picture research to retail buying.

CASE STUDY

Name: Emma Hanham
Job role: Production Secretary, BBC
Qualifications: *Degree:* BA Art History and Theology (2.i), University of Bristol *A levels:* History of Art, History, Theology

Emma's job involves work on three programmes in the BBC's Documentaries Department. Currently these include one current affairs programme and two docusoaps.

'The work is administrative and mainly based in my office – but I do get to go out sometimes. If I'm out with the film crew, once the cameras have started rolling I act as an extra pair of eyes for directors. They can't see what is going on out of camera range whereas I can make sure that the camera crew are not going to bump into anyone and that no accidents happen. I might also have to get permissions. On a filming trip at Heathrow Airport one of my duties was to run after passers-by who had been included in shots, explain this to them and obtain their permission to be filmed.

'It is an incredibly interesting job. I sort out everything connected with filming, from clearing rights to use a piece of music, to making sure that we can definitely get into places and keeping an eye on the budget. Most of my days are spent on the administrative work connected with programmes. Today, for instance, my first job was to finalise the arrangements for some foreign filming. I started by briefing the camera crew and sound manager. (My manager knows all the good camera men and women and she had made sure she got the ones she wanted.) I had already organised their flights and hotels, so I now had to give them their tickets and some currency.

'Then I moved on to work for a future programme. I was organising permission to use a piece of music. That meant clearing copyright with the owner and agreeing a payment. When I wasn't on the phone I got on with typing up the transcript of some interviews that had been recorded earlier for another programme. I have to be very organised. I spend a lot of time on the phone – and on my computer.

'This job is a first step for me. To get into the BBC in any capacity is very competitive. It is a question of getting a foot in the door. Now that I am here I shall watch for an opportunity to move into research. One way is to do my own research first – do some background work and try to find a producer who would give me a trial as an inexperienced researcher.'

Emma liked all her A level subjects equally, so chose her degree course as a means of keeping up her interest in all of them. She had vague ideas that she was 'heading toward an arty, media slot – something creative or involving writing' and had organised her school work experience placement in an art gallery. She then, as she says, bounced cheerfully through university until her last year, when she began to think seriously about a career. It was here that she benefited from an excellent course organised by her careers advisory service. She attended a three-day course on the media, in which students working in small groups did role play exercises as imaginary journalists and also wrote an eight-minute television drama piece. Their efforts were judged by Nick Parkes (of *Wallace and Grommit* fame) and a presenter from BBC Bristol.

Emma knew now what she wanted to do and wrote to BBC Bristol asking to do some unpaid work experience. She was accepted and worked there on a wildlife project. 'I researched material in their library, did odd jobs but, most important, saw how things were done and met producers.' Two years later Emma landed herself a permanent job. Before then she did more unpaid work, this time on a national magazine (and gained useful experience in writing pieces for their promotions department), spent several months travelling, did a secretarial course, then settled down to a job hunt.

'I did several temporary jobs for an agency, events organisation at Olympia and Earls Court. The best thing I did was to enrol with the temp agency. They had me down for television work and had access to vacancies I would never have found by myself. Eventually, they found me the job here.'

Skills Emma gained on her degree course

- Essay writing – which easily translates into report writing.
- 'The ability to focus my mind and to narrow down ideas.'
- Research skills: how to sort the relevant from the irrelevant.

Emma's advice

'Get a good class of degree in a subject you enjoy. This impresses employers in my career area as much as one of the apparently relevant degrees. However, when I graduated I was a well-rounded person but not immediately employable. It is essential to gain some work-related skills, whether you do so during your time at university or afterwards as I did. I learned all my administrative skills on my secretarial course and in my various office jobs. My temp jobs also taught me how to use different computer systems. If you are aiming for a career in the media it is essential to have some relevant work experience behind you. This will nearly always have to be unpaid – so you will need to have earned or saved some money to support yourself while doing it.'

CAREER NOTE

Getting into broadcasting is notoriously difficult. Few companies run formal training schemes, other than for news journalists. Some form of work experience is essential – and many successful applicants begin as Emma did by getting a foot in the door in an administrative capacity.

CASE STUDY

Name: Lisa Kelly
Job role: Department Manager, John Lewis (department store)
Qualifications: *Degree:* BA History of Art with History (2.i), University of Bristol *A levels:* Social and Environmental Biology, English Language, Social and Economic History

Lisa had always enjoyed art – and if she had felt that she had any talent for the practical side, would have taken it as a fourth A level. So when it came to degree course choice it seemed natural to choose history of art – to indulge her creative side – together with history, which was her strongest subject. She also had the idea of a career using art history in mind and was thinking about work in art dealing, valuation, gallery management or museum curatorship. To her surprise, history of art was not creative. It was similar to history, which formed 25% of the course.

'I loved the style of work. I loved the opportunity to do my own research and spent hours in the library doing the sort of work that had not been possible at A level – reading stacks of information and evaluating other people's opinions. Some of the topics I just hadn't anticipated at all, like the influence some way-out philosophers had had on French painters and how others had been influenced by Wagner's music. In the first year the two subjects were quite unrelated but from then, when I had more choice, I deliberately chose options on the history side that would complement the history of art.'

Lisa's career plans received a jolt almost as soon as she started her course. 'I realised that there were limited openings in galleries unless you were rich enough to own one or had friends who collected art, and the idea of working at the bottom of the heap for years in a national gallery or museum – until I got a chance of promotion – was not appealing.'

She was finding her academic work so interesting, however – and so time consuming – that she had no time to give to thinking about alternative careers: 'Suddenly I was in my third year and beginning to panic, thinking, "What am I going to do?" ' So Lisa went to her careers service hoping to find an answer. She tried everything, she says: completed computerised questionnaires, attended a presentation on careers in the media – which appeared every bit as competitive as art history – but, other than deciding against a postgraduate course, was no further forward. She then decided to concentrate on finals.

'I really did work very hard to get my degree and I was so wrapped up in finals that I felt sure I wouldn't come over well at milk round interviews. I simply had no time to spend on preparing elaborate presentations.' After graduating Lisa decided to take time out to travel and took a full-time job in a restaurant to finance it. She had worked as a waitress during her degree course and was fortunate in having no debts to repay. She loved the work, earned a good salary through 'incredible tips' and impressed the managers so much that she was soon promoted to supervisory level. This increased her confidence and she felt ready to leave and manage another restaurant. She enjoyed this too – and the travelling never happened.

Three years later Lisa realised that this was not what she wanted to do for the rest of her life: 'There was no intellectual stimulus. I was not using my brain and the company I was with gave me no long-term security. There was no sick pay or pension scheme.' She went back to Bristol University's careers service. There she analysed her own skills and found that they matched those required in retailing, while the John Lewis Partnership (JLP) matched her personal requirement to work for an employer with principles that agreed with her own. Lisa applied to the Bristol store and was invited to attend an assessment day. She prepared well by watching the JLP video in the careers information room, reading about the company and visiting some of the stores. Doing this helped in the interviews, but it was her previous experience that helped in the selection exercises.

'There were several during the day. In one we all in turn had to pick a card with the name of a charity on it and give our reasons to the rest of the group for recommending that JLP should make a donation to it. Mine was a particularly obscure one and I had to think on my feet fast. I was the only candidate that day to go forward to the next stage. I honestly don't think I would have been chosen if I had applied during my final year at university.'

During the second stage interviews Lisa was asked the obvious sorts of questions, such as 'What are we looking for in a manager?' and more searching ones, concentrating on her personal skills. She was also asked to take to the interview something that demonstrated a strong interest or commitment to a spare-time activity. She chose to take photographs of furniture that she had painted as a hobby. Lisa was chosen to join JLP's management development programme at the Cribbs Causeway store near Bristol. She was placed in a department to work as a selling assistant and given a training diary with targets to complete. The aim was to experience all aspects of sales work and to reach junior management level in one year. Lisa did so in three months.

'I worked my socks off again, spent evenings working on my assignments and preparing presentations and set my own targets for each month. I found my degree training was very useful in helping me to write concise reports.'

In her present job Lisa is in charge of half of ladies' fashions and has a team of 30 staff. Three are section managers – one responsible for lingerie, swimwear and nightwear, another for outerwear and the third for administration. The rest of the staff are sales advisers or, as JLP calls them, partners. (Lisa is a management partner.) What does she do in a typical day?

'The first thing is to check staffing levels. I need to know that I have enough assistants to cover each section and will already have planned for holidays or training courses. If people are absent through sickness or emergencies I'll have to go to the staff office and ask for help from other departments. I meet the section managers next and ask whether they have any problems, then I tackle my in-tray. I put my memos in priority order and decide an order for acting on them. I think that years of working in a small space in a library have helped me to be a very neat worker. I hate a messy desk! For the rest of the day I spend regular periods on the sales floor to check whether the team is having any difficulties, monitor customer service and make sure that I take time to chat to all my staff. In my time off the floor I could be holding training sessions, thinking out strategies to develop sales, meeting with my managing director to discuss my results, or maybe planning some evening in-store events. I have to constantly analyse sales and wastage figures (wastage means goods that are damaged or lost in transit) and think of ways to improve them. I always have some kind of project on the go, for myself on aspects of running this department or perhaps for the managing director on ways of pushing the business forward and making our store stand out. It is my job to make things happen.'

What does she like about her job?

'The sheer variety. No two days are ever the same. Managing a team of people. And the fact that in this company I can manage in a way that I like. People are treated with dignity. There is a genuine democracy, with partners' views asked for all the time.'

The skills Lisa gained from her degree . . .

- Time management.
- Self-discipline: 'I had six hours of lectures each week. I had to motivate myself to go to the library and work.'
- Ability to handle paperwork and to prioritise.
- Decision-making ability: 'I learned to do my own research and to analyse. I am sure that being a graduate helps me in the strategic planning side of my job.'

... and from work experience

- Ability to work in a team.
- Leadership.
- Willingness to delegate: 'It's difficult to learn to let go and to trust your staff to do things rather than to keep tight control yourself.'

Lisa's advice

'I would love to have been born knowing that I wanted to be a vet. I wasn't. If you have no burning career ambition, resist all pressure to do a "useful" subject and do something that you want to do. You will be surprised at the number of skills you gain from doing a subject that you enjoy doing.'

CAREER NOTE

Most of the major retailers run graduate training schemes. They vary in length from company to company but typically include periods working as an assistant in different selling departments, as a supervisor and in off-the-floor departments such as human resources, marketing or accounts. While training, graduates usually attend short courses with other management trainees and are often given projects to complete.

9 Leisure and Tourism

OVERVIEW

This is a comparative newcomer to the ranks of degree subjects and is usually available at universities that have a tradition of running vocational subjects (i.e. those relating to particular career areas). However, taking the course does not confine you to working within the travel/leisure industries: it's an excellent base if this is what you want to do, but you can move in many different directions after graduation.

WHAT WILL YOU GAIN FROM STUDYING LEISURE AND TOURISM?

You will obtain a broad knowledge of many different disciplines and can often choose to specialise in a specific area (or areas) of interest. The topics covered include environmental issues, business courses, marketing and branding, so this is a good basis for all kinds of jobs. In addition, it is often offered as a joint degree. This means that you can study it alongside a course that dovetails with it (heritage studies with leisure for example, languages or geography with tourism, business studies with both) or combine it with the study of another area entirely, thus widening your options even further. It is a practical subject, so you will undertake field trips and hands-on research, such as carrying out surveys, and you will gain expertise in using statistics and statistical programs. Much of the coursework will be project-based, often in groups, culminating in reports and oral presentations, so you can add these to the raft of skills that you should acquire. You'll study – and see first hand in some cases – other cultures, countries and ways of life, which can only be beneficial in expanding your views and knowledge of current issues.

Key themes in tourism at the moment are sustainability and care of the environment – these are likely to have very far-reaching applications in numerous job sectors as the 21st century progresses. Within the specialist arena of tourism itself, all sorts of niche areas are opening up: eco- and agro-tourism, for instance; 'extreme', adventure and wilderness tourism and sports tourism. Even in times of economic difficulty, people will always want to spend time and money on travel and on disparate leisure activities, so there is no shortage of possibilities for future employment.

CAREER POSSIBILITIES

When we think of careers for graduates of this discipline, we tend to envisage those in the public eye – perhaps those that we have experienced as consumers. These include holiday tour representative, travel agent and air cabin crew. Many graduates from leisure and tourism degrees enter these kinds of jobs, as do people from unrelated courses. These roles do not always demand a university-level education, but are very popular because they offer the prospect of time abroad, enjoying the sun (or snow) while working and perhaps developing one's own leisure interests while being paid. The downsides are that they can be short term and, seasonal although some people like the variety and flexibility that this brings. Apart from these obvious customer-facing roles, there are also many 'behind the scenes' opportunities in leisure and tourism: researching, developing and marketing new destinations, for instance.

Leisure and tourism may also include heritage management. This is growing increasingly important in the UK and other countries as we become aware of the need to protect, preserve and interpret our history, culture and architecture and make it accessible to those who may not otherwise be exposed to it, e.g. aiming to increase the appeal of museums to non-traditional visitors and setting up oral history projects before traditional ways of life are lost or memories dissipated.

A final strand of this subject is sports science and its offshoots such as sport and leisure studies. Again, this is aimed at broadening the appeal of physical activity, making it more relevant and exciting and encouraging people to incorporate it into their lifestyles. Sports development – working with specific people or communities – is a growing career area. Sometimes two or more of these disciplines may come together: Claire McNicholls, our first case study, mentions an interest in sports tourism, for instance.

GRADUATE DESTINATIONS

Perhaps because leisure and tourism is a new (but expanding) field of study, HESA does not collect any figures for careers entered by graduates who have studied this subject. Therefore it is difficult to identify any over-arching destinations for these students. But maybe this sums up the subject's appeal – the world's your oyster.

The two graduates in the following case studies studied tourism at the same college a year apart, but both their courses and their careers have followed very separate paths.

CASE STUDY

Name: Claire McNicholls
Job role: Community Information Officer, London Borough of Richmond upon Thames
Qualifications: *Degree:* BA Tourism and Management (2.i), St Mary's University College, Strawberry Hill, Twickenham *A levels:* Geography, Travel and Tourism

As is evident from her A level choice, Claire had a long-standing interest in this area. However, in one way, she found the Travel and Tourism A level a drawback because she was re-treading old ground in the first year of her degree. Nonetheless, once she got into her stride she found her time at Strawberry Hill fascinating and enjoyable.

'The course was fun and gave me know-how that has been directly useful in my current job. It wasn't just reading and theory – I saw how what I learned could be put into practice. For instance, we had to look at London as a tourist destination, we did tourism planning and we undertook research that is still applicable to what I'm doing here.

I chose to take an optional work experience placement at Osterley House and Park, a local historical attraction, and while there I carried out a survey into interpretation methods, which has now been adapted by Ham House, another nearby tourist destination.'

During her degree, Claire spent weekends working at Hounslow Tourist Information Centre (TIC) and this supplemented the practical aspects of her studies and helped her realise that she enjoyed working with the public. When she finished at St Mary's, she was not entirely sure what direction to take, but a temporary job in data inputting clarified her ideas, besides improving her computer skills. She also did short-term work at the British Museum as a visitor host and box office clerk for a busy exhibition. 'I'm sure my degree and previous customer service experience was instrumental in getting that role, and, in turn, having such a prestigious name on my CV has led on to other things.' When Claire came to look for a more permanent nook, her education and experience were very much in her favour, so much so that the interview for her present post 'was more like a chat'.

Claire loves both the variety and the autonomy she now has. 'I operate across two departments – education and environment – and in two different locations, the TIC and the library. It's not just desk-based; there's lots of independence and I can develop my own projects. I get out and about, for instance staffing our stand at the May Fair, and, a year into the job, I'm already supervising other staff. I also do a lot of research to keep the council website updated with both community events and tourist information, covering the whole borough.' She's developed web-writing skills and is able to use her creative side. 'I was thrilled recently when someone who had been surfing the site said that I had inspired her to visit Richmond.'

She is enthusiastic about all the training that she is able to access. 'We can do orientation and familiarisation trips – I've just been visiting the London Docklands to see what's happening there – and my employers will pay for me to take qualifications such as the European Computer Driving Licence.'

What future does Claire see in this aspect of tourism? 'The potential is huge. I took this up because I wanted to get involved and to promote my community. The 2012 Olympics is a fabulous opportunity for us and it particularly attracts me because I'm keen on sport and am doing a personal trainer qualification in my own time. Sports tourism is developing constantly, so maybe I'll get involved with that. I'm ambitious and have already told my boss I have my eye on her job!

It's a big sector, always changing and very dynamic. I can go off in any direction I want. I'm in the most perfect job I could have.'

Skills Claire gained on her degree course . . .

- Report writing, proofreading, attention to detail: 'There was a lot of detailed qualitative and quantitative analysis needed.'
- Working in teams: 'I was proud of pulling together various group initiatives and it's something that's important now when I'm part of various small project teams.'
- 'Increasing my understanding of such a wide range of subjects.'
- Presentation skills and using PowerPoint effectively.

. . . and from student life in general

Confidence!

Claire's advice

'Choose a course that interests you and, before you apply, talk to people who have done the course and been to the university. Look at the pastoral care that you receive – it was a small college and our tutors were always there for us. I didn't move away from home, which goes against the received wisdom, but it worked for me. In fact, I think I got this current job because I was local. And definitely get some work experience as part of your studies or in your free time. When it comes to finding graduate-type work, keep plugging away. It takes a while.'

CASE STUDY

Name: Katie MacKichan
Job role: Acting Assistant Manager, Early Learning Centre, and part-time research assistant
Qualifications: *Degree:* BA Tourism and Geography (2.i), St Mary's University College, Strawberry Hill, Twickenham *A levels:* Geography, Travel and Tourism

Katie followed Claire to St Mary's University College, but took geography with her tourism qualification. 'The two areas overlapped sometimes, which did mean that you learned the same thing twice, but we were all able to tailor the course to our own interests. I had enjoyed human geography at A level and this was a way to expand that content across two disciplines. I think the degree pushed me and helped me to see what my strengths were.'

Unlike Claire, she wasn't able to find a work experience placement, which was initially disappointing but enabled her to take a web design module. 'This turned out to be so interesting that I extended it into my third year. It's highly transferable and very handy now in one of my jobs.' Rather than write a dissertation, Katie opted to do a research essay, and this allowed her to investigate an area close to her heart: ecotourism.

The best thing about doing tourism? 'Definitely the field trip to Grenada – and not just for the obvious reasons either! We had to pay for it ourselves, but it was well worth it. Seeing another culture and tourist infrastructure really hits home and makes what you are studying very real.'

When she came to leave St Mary's, Katie decided to take a job unrelated to her course. Throughout her university career, she had worked part-time at the Early Learning Centre and was promoted to a senior sales position. 'I really loved it here and colleagues and management were very supportive, so I took on more hours after graduation and soon effectively became a junior manager.'

Katie is enthusiastic about retail, despite the fact that it can be physically tiring and occasionally stressful. 'It's not just what you see when you're in a store – serving on the till, etc. I thrive on the customer interaction, plus we actually get to see some of our clients grow up! I love running a team, briefing them, helping them to hit targets and playing to each individual's strengths while improving their weaknesses. I like having to make decisions even if it is often under pressure, such as arranging staff cover at short notice. I have a finger in all kinds of pies: merchandising, setting up new lines, arranging promotions, interviewing and training new recruits, looking after payroll. It can be daunting but I've certainly been able to demonstrate professionalism.'

And Katie hasn't totally moved away from what she studied: 'I got a passion for sustainability from university, and three days a week I do research for an author who is writing a book on aspects of this. It's called *Climb The Green Ladder: Make Your Company and Career More Sustainable,* is published by Whiley and looks at how companies of all sizes can do their bit for the environment. A soon as I saw the advert,

I knew it was just me. I matched the skills on my CV to what they were seeking – my degree had given me a lot of what was needed. I research potential interviewees and set up meetings between them and the writer. I also do some of the interviews myself. Then the hard work of transcribing and editing these and updating the database kicks in. It's made the most of my web courses.'

Katie eventually sees herself merging these two contrasting strands of her working life. 'I would love to get into corporate social responsibility and my different jobs have enabled me to see both sides of the coin and given me a foot in two camps.'

The skills Katie gained from her degree . . .

- Numerical, analytical and logical abilities.
- Team leadership as part of fieldwork.
- IT – 'which now plays an important part in all aspects of my work. Formatting and structuring reports, ditto.'

. . . and from university life in general

- Communication.
- Working independently – 'which, again, is essential for what I do now.'
- Friends.
- A chance to see the world.

Katie's advice

'Don't be put off by people saying that vocational degrees are not academic. I worked just as hard as people on "traditional" academic courses. Tourism gave me the opportunity to study so many things – business management, marketing and world affairs, apart from what I've already mentioned. Do what interests you.'

Like Claire, she feels that big isn't always best. 'Don't feel that you have to go a large university – a smaller place can be more friendly and equally educational.'

10 Modern Languages

OVERVIEW

We are frequently told that the British are very bad at learning languages and that people of other nationalities are at an advantage through their willingness to learn one if not more foreign languages. So surely any UK student proficient in languages should find employers queuing up to offer them jobs? Well, no, unfortunately. The point is that languages are skills. They are an asset but rarely a career in themselves.

WHAT WILL YOU GAIN FROM STUDYING LANGUAGES?

In addition to specific linguistic expertise, language students acquire a good many more skills. They are first and foremost communicators. They spend large amounts of time speaking, discussing and making presentations. They can communicate well in writing. They have the general essay-writing skills of any arts graduate but they have also learned to be very precise in their use of language.

Translation calls at the same time for accuracy and creative use of language. The text translated must be a true reflection of the original but it must also sound as though it had been written in the new language. This requires excellent skill in manipulating the English language. Using foreign languages requires further accuracy and care (all those grammar rules and the verb endings that must agree). Many languages graduates use their skills in careers where attention to detail is required, such as law, journalism and publishing. Others become computer programmers – a job that demands logical ability.

Language graduates have usually spent a period abroad. The added independence they have gained from this experience plus the understanding of other cultures makes them valuable to many employers. Encouragingly, one or two people who feature as case studies in this book refer to the period spent in other countries as especially valuable in their personal development. Most students seem to enjoy it, but not all of them see its applicability to the wider world of work. Diane Appleton, a careers adviser at the University of Liverpool, certainly felt that the modern linguists whom she met were not making the most of their time abroad when they applied for graduate jobs back home. As a result she set up a programme to help them reflect on the skills they acquired while away and to support them while they were out of the country. Employers such as Aldi and Deloitte contributed to this and, hopefully, it will help those graduates when they are job hunting. It's something that you, too, should bear in mind if you are studying languages. It should be a selling point when you are drafting a CV or making an application.

CAREER POSSIBILITIES

The only directly related careers are teaching, interpreting and translating. Of these, interpreting (the spoken word) is the smallest. Very, very few people indeed earn a living through interpreting alone. Most combine it with translating (the written word) and even then may have to supplement their earnings by teaching. Most translating jobs are freelance and demand a detailed knowledge of at least one (and preferably more) occupational areas such as health or engineering. Many would-be translators pick this up on a master's course, but they do report that it's tough going. It's a help to have a second or third foreign language up your sleeve and not necessarily one of the usual suspects such as French or Spanish. Instead Asian, middle Eastern and eastern European languages are much in demand. Other postgraduate options include diplomas in public service interpreting and in niche areas such as subtitling.

However, in some sectors modern linguists are extremely employable. As we saw in Chapter 2, languages are now considered a desirable baseline skill by many graduate recruiters. There are many careers in the field of business and commerce where this is an advantage – from banking to insurance, marketing to law, accountancy to purchasing and distribution to logistics management, not to mention the more obvious areas of the Civil Service (including the diplomatic service), the European Union institutions, travel, tourism and hospitality.

The Civil Service is traditionally an employer of linguists – particularly in the various departments of the European Commission (where a prerequisite for entry is the ability to speak a second European language) and the surveillance services, such as GCHQ and MI5. The latter don't often look for European languages, although they may seize on someone with a degree in these subjects and retrain them in other less widely available dialects.

GRADUATE DESTINATIONS

'What do graduates do?' shows that most language graduates move into the same category of administrative work as other arts graduates and in roughly the same proportion. A fuller breakdown can be found in Chapter 3.

CASE STUDY

Name: Sophie van Maurik
Jobe role: Marketing/Administrative Assistant, Strategic Real Estate Advisors and Asset Managers
Qualifications: *Degree:* BA French (2.i), Bristol University
A levels: Geography, Art, French

Sophie 'really enjoyed' her student days and especially her year abroad in France: 'I thought the degree was good because it was so wide. We covered French literature, politics and history as well as language, although that was obviously a major part of the course. We had to do lots of translation and I chose to take Spanish as a subsidiary during my first year. During my third year, I spent nine months as a language assistant in a school in the south-west of France. Although I still think that a business placement might have been an even better way to improve my spoken and written skills, it was a fun time. There were lots of other students in the area and

I really got to know the country. My language improved no end: the teachers at the school would only speak to me in French both socially and at work. When my time there came to an end I worked in the Alps for the summer and, again, spoke only French.

It was quite a shock for all of us to return to Bristol, and the fourth year involved a lot of hard studying. I was looking to the future and applied for a few things before graduating, on a fairly random basis. I had no real ideas about what I wanted to do, though I knew I wasn't interested in translation or teaching. I didn't feel that I had to use French in a job – it would have been a bonus, but wasn't vital.'

Sophie went for one job coaching the long-term unemployed, but it was felt that she lacked the necessary experience. Marketing was another possibility that she had considered: she investigated it further and then met someone involved in it via a jobs/social networking website. One thing led to another and she was offered her current post.

'This is my first proper job and I've never been in a business environment before, so I'm learning a lot. We specialise in advising high-end clients about real estate. We did cover a short module in French for business at university, so the vocabulary has come in handy, but I had little commercial awareness. It's a small company and all my colleagues are good at showing me the ropes. In my admin role, I assist one of the senior specialist advisers when he is in the office or preparing for a company trip. I also order materials, liaise with suppliers and printers, and do some printing and binding of marketing resources myself. I am responsibe for the upkeep of the press book and the website – that means a great deal of liaison with the developers to have amends made.

Occasionally I may get involved with editing documents, presentations and photo books, as well as sorting out arrangements for meetings and overseeing travel arrangements. A lot of my work involves calling clients on the phone. I only use my languages if I'm dealing with a French client, but I knew when I took the position that this would be the case. As and when I move on, I hope that my degree will come into its own – maybe I'll work for a French firm next.'

The skills Sophie gained from her degree . . .

■ Teamwork skills, including leading a group in a presentation that counted for 10% of the final mark: 'It was horrible at the time, but a good learning experience.'

- Self-confidence when speaking French: 'We had all changed a lot by the time we came back from our year abroad.'
- Presentation skills as part of student-led seminars.

. . . and from university life in general

Time management: 'Contact hours were low, so you were expected to manage your own study and put in the hours needed.'

Sophie's advice

'My degree had a lot of variety, but, looking back, joint honours or taking an extra language in depth might have been advantageous. The time abroad was pivotal and I made sure that I maximised this on my CV – for instance I spelled out that I'd taken lessons by myself.'

CASE STUDY

Name: Ben Harrison
Job role: Reservations Consultant, Abercrombie and Kent
Qualifications: *Degree:* BA French (2.i), Newcastle University
A levels: French, German, Geography, General Studies

'The course was fun for all sorts of reasons – one being that men formed only 10% of the intake! But it was a varied and balanced degree, a mix of academic, practical and supplementary courses. My major was French, my minor German. For me, the film and literature modules stood out and I think I learned more in the theory classes than in the actual oral sessions.'

Like most language students, Ben spent much of the third year abroad, in this case in France. 'I should have gone to Germany as well, but my interest in German had dwindled by that point. I was a language assistant in a school. I still count it as one of the best years of my life. We lived on school premises and our teaching was concentrated into a few days a week so we had plenty of free time. It was my first time away from the UK on my own and I picked up a lot of life skills.'

By the time Ben graduated, a flatmate had pointed out a job with the holiday firm Vacances Franco Britannique (VFB) in the Alps: his language skills helped him secure this. Despite a mountain bike accident that restricted his travels for a while, he then took off for Australia for nearly a year. 'I did bits and pieces of work while I was there – including door-to-door selling, which stood me in good stead later.'

All good things come to an end, and when Ben returned home, he was unsure what to do next. His time in France had made him aware that he didn't want to teach, and, while he had toyed with the idea of translating, he realised that it was necessary to be virtually bilingual in order to do this professionally. So he contacted VFB again and went to work in their Cheltenham office, selling holiday cottages, *gites* and holidays. 'I used my French, but in a pretty limited way – just basic vocabulary really.'

The travel bug bit again and Ben took off round the world with a companion to Central and North America, the Pacific, New Zealand and back to Australia before ending up in Cheltenham again. 'I wanted to stay in the Cheltenham area, but was keen to do something slightly different, so I became a reservations consultant for Abercrombie and Kent, an up-market tour operator. I started out in the European and Middle East section and now I've moved to dealing with Africa and the Indian Ocean area, severing virtually all my links with the French language, except when contacting places like Mauritius and the Seychelles.

'A lot of what I do is intensive phone work with clients and with our contacts abroad. Clients will see our brochures and come to me with an idea of what sort of holiday they want – this may be very definite or pretty vague. I help them put together a tailored itinerary based on their interests and their budget. I suppose this was slightly easier when I was specialising on the European side – more complications can come up when you're trying to arrange a multicentre vacation in Africa! I'm not sure what part my degree played in all this – it gave me good general communication abilities, I think. You do need those to build up a rapport over the phone, whatever language you're speaking. I think what helped me most was the door-to-door sales work in Australia – after that, everything else was a breeze!'

Ben likes being in the tourism sector, but concedes that it's not a field where he will ever make a lot of money. 'There are perks and bonuses of course. I get to do site visits abroad – often these are to places that I wouldn't necessarily have thought of myself, but I wouldn't have missed them now I have gone there. And I can make the most of industry concessions and offers when I go on holiday myself. For instance, I won a trip to Oman in a trade competition and I recently went to the Galapagos Islands, which would have required a lot more cash if it wasn't for the discount that I can claim.'

The skills Ben gained from his degree . . .

- 'Languages obviously – and if I don't use French much now, it was what got me into my job in the first place.'
- Communication: 'Because I'm at home with language, I find it easy to paint a picture of a holiday to a client over the phone and to succinctly sum up what's available.'
- Confidence: 'which really came from my year in France.'

. . . and from university life in general

Fun and forging good friendships.

Ben's advice

'Looking back, I could have used more of the facilities and opportunities I had at university. In terms of giving any tips about careers with languages, I think it's a good idea to pursue other subjects, and skills and interests as well, rather than just relying on linguistic abilities. Classmates who combined their languages with an interest in law, business or economics often went on to the best paid jobs.'

CASE STUDY

Name: Victoria Weaver
Job role: Barrister
Qualifications: *Degree:* BA French and Spanish (2.i), University of Exeter; Graduate Diploma in Law, Bar Vocational Course, both at the College of Law, London Bloomsbury *A levels:* French, Spanish, Music, General Studies

'I went to Exeter because I preferred a campus university, but it was a good choice whatever my original reasons! It was split 50/50 between the two languages, though the content was very different. French was quite literary, Spanish more cultural with a wider mix of options. I spent time in both France and Spain. My French placement, through the university, was as a language assistant in a school, dealing with children of upper primary/lower secondary age. I was based in a fairly deprived location and it was often taxing, but it had its moments! I financed my stay in Spain myself and used the two months to take a Spanish course in Granada: it definitely improved my spoken language.'

Having spent a year abroad, what changes did Victoria notice on returning to Exeter? 'All my peer group fell back into their old lives. I don't think we had altered, but it was strange finding that our friends on other degrees had graduated and moved on. That was the only downside to being away for an extended period.'

Victoria had already decided at the A level stage that she wanted to become a barrister, so she knew that this would entail studying law for two years after graduation. She decided to take 12 months out before embarking on this part of her plans. 'I'd had enough of studying for a while. I worked for a short time and used this to fund a trip to South America. The Spanish spoken there is very different from what I'd learned in Europe, so it was occasionally difficult to understand what was going on!'

Back in the UK, Victoria found the Graduate Diploma in Law (GDL) very intensive. 'Much longer hours than you get on an arts degree. I didn't feel that it was too intellectually challenging, but there was a lot to do and it wasn't easy to cram everything in.' She was well aware that entry to the Bar was – and remains – notoriously tough. 'I did wonder how realistic I was being and looked at the possibility of becoming a trainee solicitor as well, but after some mini pupillages [specialist work experience in barristers' chambers], I knew that this was what I wanted to do, so I just decided to go for it.'

The next stage of her training, the Bar Vocational Course (BVC) was, she thought, less demanding than the GDL. 'I saw it a means to an end, just a necessary requirement on the road to becoming fully qualified. It was very competitive – we were all after the same small pool of jobs – but I enjoyed it and learning advocacy skills was great fun. Nonetheless, it can't mirror reality and I learned more once I obtained a pupillage.' Pupillage is the final part of training and is another hurdle to negotiate: the application form and the interview process are challenging and not everyone succeeds. Victoria was one of the lucky ones, though she did receive a few rejections en route and cautions others to be ready for this.

Now a fully fledged barrister specialising in criminal law, she points out 'It's not like the TV! It has its ups and downs – you can often not tell whether you are going to be busy or quiet and you may have to get work done very quickly. You're in court all morning – sometimes all day. Then you might come back to chambers to catch up on paper work and go on well into the evening to prepare for the next case, which may not be notified until after 4 pm. You can be working at weekends too and have to forego extended holidays, as you'll miss out on cases. Hours are long and can be stressful, but I feel more in control of my time now than when I was doing my pupillage and at everyone's beck and call.'

Looking to the future, Victoria hopes to take on increasingly challenging cases. 'Most barristers are self-employed, so when you're a junior like myself, you have to work at building up your practice and your reputation.'

The skills Victoria gained from her degree . . .

- The Criminal Bar looks for well-rounded individuals with life experience, so studying languages and living in different countries was a help in this respect.
- 'I'm unlikely to use languages in this type of legal work – unlike a City solicitor whose language skills may be instrumental in obtaining a training contract. But I do feel that my degree gave me good all-round communication skills, and that's vital for my job.'

. . . and from university life in general

- Independence.
- Time management.
- Life skills.

Victoria's advice

'If you're interested in becoming a lawyer, doing a non-relevant degree shouldn't hinder you, though it will add an extra year to your studies. For me, languages were enjoyable and meant going outside the UK, broadening my horizons, and I felt that more than compensated for the intensive nature of the GDL.

It's definitely a plus to have experience of things outside law and beyond university: I'd particularly recommend voluntary work and travel. Recruiters look for any extras that you can offer! Enjoy yourself before you start your career as a barrister because it's hard work and difficult to take time off. If you do achieve your ambition, beware of exhaustion and plan your workload as much as possible.'

CAREER NOTE

There are two branches of the legal profession in England, Wales and Northern Ireland. Solicitors advise clients on business, criminal and personal matters and can generally represent them only in the lower courts. Barristers have less client contact and can defend or prosecute cases across the entire court system. Most barristers are self-employed and rely on cases being brought to them by solicitors. In Scotland, a similar system prevails, but barristers are called advocates. Britain's offshore islands have a different structure again, but most lawyers working there train on the UK mainland.

To qualify in England and Wales, if, like Victoria, you don't have a law degree, the Graduate Diploma in Law brings you up to speed on the core subjects that you'll need. The next and final part of academic training is taken by both law and non-law graduates. At this point they have to decide whether they want to go to the Bar, in which case they take the BVC as Victoria did. If they prefer to become solicitors, they enrol on the Legal Practice Course (LPC). In Scotland and Northern Ireland, similar arrangements apply, but it is less usual to come from a non-law background. For further information, see Trotman's *Law Uncovered*.

11 Music

OVERVIEW

A career in music has a lot in common with the other performing arts, which are covered in Chapter 12. It might be a good idea to look at this chapter for any points that these related fields have in common.

Two of our case studies – husband and wife Andrew and Lindsey Ashwin – have forged successful careers in music, but they illustrate perfectly the sort of lifestyle that often accompanies this – freelance and portfolio work, both of which are discussed in Chapter 1. Also in Chapter 1, you will find Jim Lockey, a popular music graduate who is a self-employed director of a small record label. If you intend to follow their lead, be prepared to face the sort of difficulties that all three graduates overcame, but take heart from their obvious enthusiasm!

Although there are a growing number of degrees covering popular music, they are not necessary to succeed in this field. Many rock stars actually come from an art school background – Eric Clapton and Jarvis Cocker being just two of these. Others may have done an academic degree or decided not to continue their education after school. What is needed if you intend to be a performer is 'making yourself visible'. This requires persistence and you could start out by playing in small venues – churches, clubs, pubs – to sparse audiences. Perseverance is the name of the game. Reputations are not built overnight!

WHAT WILL YOU GAIN FROM STUDYING MUSIC?

Beyond the obvious music-related careers, what can graduates in this subject offer employers? They are good team players

and often very innovative. They usually have an excellent
eye for detail, they think logically and frequently have a
high level of numeracy – strong mathematical abilities often
go hand in hand with musical talent. So many traditional
graduate employers might welcome those with a music
degree, even though, at first glance, they appear to have little
in common. One student with both a BA and an MA in
music successfully entered high-level employment with
a major player in international finance by selling all the
above skills combined with one less obvious talent: he had
organised and promoted his own concert tours on a scant
budget for several years and made a large profit. This showed
a high level of commercial awareness and the company
snapped him up.

Lisa Whistlecroft, Deputy Director of PALATINE, the
Higher Education Academy's subject centre for supporting
learning and teaching in dance, drama and music, flags up
the following skills on top of the ones already mentioned:
'*Musicians are articulate and good communicators. They
have confidence and tend to be well organized. They can be
both leaders and followers. Often they are excellent spatially
and are strong on analysis and logic. IT is just one area where
they might make an impact.*'

CAREER POSSIBILITIES

Performance is not the only direction in which music
graduates can go: there are opportunities in administration
with record companies, orchestras and music publishers.
Sound recording and record production are also possible, but
they are hard nuts to crack unless you have built up expertise
and contacts while at college.

Lisa Whistlecroft has seen music graduates enter all sorts
of careers, from retail management to MI5. However, she
thinks that sometimes they are not very good at making
employers aware of what they have to offer. '*People
identify themselves by the instrument that they play – as
in "I'm a violinist". But most of them are not going to go
into professional careers as musicians and have all kinds of*

potential for other employment.' Lisa is aware that many people use employment destinations to show how many graduates are 'lost to music'. She debunks this way of thinking. *'I can remember one music graduate who became an accountant. This offered a comfortable 9–5 existence and the chance to earn good money. But once he left the office, he spent his free time making music – teaching privately, running an orchestra, helping with community music. Many people become school teachers for the same reason, and this is a positive thing. Music gives you the tools to stay involved with your discipline and to go on to do other things as well.'*

GRADUATE DESTINATIONS

Does the annual survey of graduate destinations in the booklet 'What do graduates do? bear out Lisa's theory? Music is included with other performing arts. It shows that the largest number of performing arts graduates (21.1%) became just what you might expect: arts, design, culture and sports professionals such as dance/gym coach and orchestra manager.

The more detailed breakdown of the destinations of performing arts graduates shows that, although 16% entered retail, catering and bar work, only 12.8% were classified as being in clerical and secretarial occupations. This compares very positively with other 'traditional' arts graduates who are often in temporary jobs to gain experience or to earn a living while making applications for 'graduate-level' jobs.

- 15.3% of the performing arts cohort entered occupations defined as 'other'. Some of these were perhaps surprising (trainee prison officer, for instance) and others were less unexpected (support worker with an arts organisation).
- 13.3% of the performing arts cohort were employed as education professionals (e.g. music teachers both in individual schools and on a peripatetic or roving basis).

(Total number of students surveyed: 8,205.)

CASE STUDY

Name: Lindsey Ashwin
Job role: Choir director, teacher of music and English as a foreign language, personal fitness trainer
Qualifications: *Degree*: BA Music (2.i), University of Birmingham, followed by a Postgraduate Certificate in Education (PGCE), Homerton College, Cambridge *A levels*: Music, Physics, Maths

To date, Lindsey has juggled an array of very different jobs and she has worked both in the UK and in Germany. How has she found her career path out so far? Let's start at the beginning.

'I thought my university course was excellent! It struck just the right balance between history, composition and performance and we could more or less tailor it to what we wanted. We were based at the university, but our performance lessons were at the highly prestigious Birmingham Conservatoire.

When I was choosing my degree I looked at universities that would let me specialise in conducting. This was something I had done with the local church choir since my early teens, when I was sent on a short course at the Royal School of Church Music.

Conducting is very close to teaching, so this was partly what led me to the PGCE. That was another good experience, even though it was hard work – lots of essays and plenty of finding out how to deal with the harsh realities of classroom management. I had approachable tutors and some strong mentoring during my two school placements. Looking back, I feel that the course itself should have been two years. Coming from a traditional classical music degree, I needed to find out about the broader subject that is offered in schools before actually learning to teach.'

After her PGCE, Lindsey successfully found employment in London, first in one large comprehensive school, before moving to another in a more senior role. Here she was able to get involved in management, in specialist areas such as vocal tuition and in teaching sixth formers. She liked the practical side of her work but felt that dealing with large groups of students, some with special needs, is not always the most appropriate way to teach music.

'Then my husband, Andrew, who is an opera singer [see case study below], was asked to perform with companies in Europe – in Belgium, then in Zurich. I decided to go with him, so took a four-week Certificate of English Language Teaching to Adults (CELTA) at International House in London. It was tough but, again, I had wonderful tutors. I actually think it might be a good course for every teacher to take as a refresher! There are lots of assignments and you have to master all the rules of grammar in order to get through.'

Once settled in Switzerland, Lindsey quickly obtained two part-time jobs teaching English. 'Working with adult learners was a new experience for me, so it was initially intimidating, especially as many of them were in senior positions in the finance industry. Then I was offered a full-time post in a school. Teaching English to teenagers in small groups is very different to delivering music lessons to classes of 30 or more in UK schools! Once I'd been there a while I took on extra responsibility and could be more creative in my approach – I found it a lot like interpreting music. The system was one of mixed age groups. Given that people sometimes stay at school there until their early twenties, I was often working with 13 year olds and 20 year olds in the same class.'

Then Lindsey's husband was offered work in Berlin and she knew that she was unlikely to find a similar TEFL set up there. The solution was obvious. She took a Level 2 Fitness Instructor qualification back in Britain! 'I went round all the gyms in Berlin and was offered work as a floor trainer and doing inductions for new members. At the same time I took my Level 3 qualification. Combined with my gym experience, this helped me find freelance personal training assignments, working one to one with clients. At the same time, I was a choir teacher at a small bilingual primary school.

In another twist, husband Andrew decided to work freelance as an opera singer in Ireland, Spain and Belgium, with the UK as a base. This meant yet another new role for Lindsey, allowing her once more to focus on her love of music, conducting and management.

'I'll be the director of choral music at a mixed state school in the East Midlands. One part of the job will be general classroom teaching. The other half will be liaising with community choirs, primary schools and doing all kinds of outreach work, which will require imagination and the ability to organise people and events. I'm really looking forward to it – and it will be nice to have a fixed salary again!'

The skills Lindsey gained from her degree . . .

- 'All the extra-curricular stuff that goes with music meant that I became very good at time management – dovetailing different sets of rehearsals, different commitments, completing assignments, etc.'

- 'Working with small ensembles helps with forging professional relationships with all sorts of people. I've used this in my various jobs when doing one-to-one personal training, for example, where you have to react to the client's situation and find out the best ways to motivate them.'
- Research abilities – always handy.

. . . and from university life in general

- Life skills such as paying bills – or discovering that if you don't, the energy supply is cut off!
- Living with other people and learning to adjust to them, however difficult this might be.
- Hitting deadlines: if you fail to hand in an essay on time, marks are deducted, which concentrates the mind wonderfully!

Lindsey's advice

'Be flexible. A job is a job, but you need to get on with your own life too. Follow things through as they happen – you can't predict where your career may go.'

CASE STUDY

Name: Andrew Ashwin
Job role: Professional opera singer, www.andrewashwin.com
Qualifications: *Degree*: BA Music (2.i), University of Birmingham, followed by postgraduate courses at the Royal College of Music and opera schools across Europe *A levels*: Music, English Language, Geography

As you might have guessed, Andrew is Lindsey's husband and they met at university. They have supported each other in their diverging career paths. In Andrew's case, a lot of advanced and intensive study right across Europe has been involved.

'I chose Birmingham because it offered a very broad music education, not too history or performance specific. I had no real thought of becoming a performer – I was just doing something that I loved; apart from the Music A level I had also taken Music Technology at AS level. The degree did give a very good grounding in performance (and I took piano and singing lessons at the Birmingham

Conservatoire, with which we were linked) but it wasn't a big part of the course. I really enjoyed all the music making possibilities that there were in the city; it was very vibrant and had a real buzz.'

It was only in his final year that Andrew specialised in performing and singing, but he still had no professional aspirations and no idea of taking up a performance career. After graduation he did some unpaid work with amateur and student opera companies and it was then that the prospect of taking his music further began to crystallise.

'I found out that it was really necessary to take a professional course in order to move forward, so I applied to the Royal Academy of Music [RAM] and the Royal College of Music [RCM]. The selection process was gruelling: two sets of auditions and one call back interview. I was offered a place at the Royal College and was lucky enough to get a scholarship too. Without that, it would have been a real struggle financially. It was a jolly good two years! Very intensive, concentrating on singing, acting and opera, learning the trade, learning about myself, finding out how the music world worked.'

Yet more study was needed if Andrew was to make the grade in the competitive world of opera. 'I applied for opera school at the RAM, the RCM and the Guildhall and didn't get any of them. That was a real blow, as everything had been going so well until then. But I saw an advert at the RCM for studying at an opera studio in Belgium. I auditioned and this time I was successful! After the RCM, which had hundreds of students, it was a bit of a culture shock to come to this tiny studio in Ghent where there were only 10 singers and two pianists. But the amount of individual attention we each got was fantastic – I think this was the best stage out of all my training. We were able to do much more exploring and experimenting than we could with a larger group.'

At this point, Andrew met an agent who would help him launch his career. As a result, he went for an audition at the Zurich Opera School. 'This was, if you like, more prestigious than Ghent, and had a link to the Zurich Opera House, which meant we got small roles there, as well as staging our own productions at the studio. I spent two years there and if it was less like family than the Belgium experience, it added a certain professionalism to my work. I really got to see how opera works, who to get to know, how to audition, the hierarchy, the system of mixing classical revivals with more modern pieces.'

All the years of study finally paid off when Andrew's agent set up an audition with the Berlin Opera, for whom he became a contract performer, whilst also guesting with the Vienna Opera.

'Now that Lindsey, my wife, has got a job in the UK, we're coming home and I'm going totally freelance, which is exciting but a bit daunting.' However, Andrew already has three contracts lined up for the next year, so the future looks good.

The skills Andrew gained from his degree . . .

- 'Musical skills obviously, but also how to behave professionally, like turning up at rehearsals on time. That doesn't come naturally at first and it can be a huge learning curve, but you have to build up good habits.'
- 'How to be a good musician. I became more rounded as a professional, a better performer, a better listener.'

. . . and from university life in general

'A sense of perspective. It was my first time away form home and I learned how to identify with and deal with people from very different backgrounds to my own.'

Andrew's advice

'Professors don't always get it right. I got average marks in my first couple of years, so if it happens to you, don't be deterred! The ambition to perform can take a knock-back at university but don't give up!

The postgraduate phase of study is very important – the amount you learn helps you to realise if you're ready and whether you're cut out for a performing career. The courses are full of quality people and you have to raise your game a couple of notches. Do try and get an agent or agency representation, though that is easier said than done – it's very hard to get your foot in the door without this.'

CASE STUDY

Name: Ursula Partridge
Job role: Technical writer and editor, corporate telecoms firm
Qualifications: *Degree*: BA Music (2.i), Cambridge University
A levels: Music, English Literature, French, Psychology, General Studies

'At the point of applying to university, I was torn between taking English literature and music. One of my teachers advised me to follow a calling. I reasoned that if I let go of music, I might let it disappear altogether, whereas with English, I still adore creative writing in my own time, while friends who did study it at university found that it inhibited their creativity.

I enjoyed the course: I was particularly good at music composition, analysis and essay writing – that's where the English came into its own! If you're good with words as well as music it really helps with structuring exam answers. I never wanted to make a career as a professional performing musician, but I did want to be surrounded by musicians. I did consider doing a PhD but thought that really it was putting my career on hold. I had done lots of work experience while at university and wanted to be some way involved in music.

Immediately after graduation, I found work with a one-man music promotion business. It wasn't what I thought: I'd imagined that I'd be swanning round after gigs with a glass of champagne. Instead there was a terrific amount of responsibility, not to mention the endless daily drudgery of basic admin. I did pretty much everything: developing a website, preparing scores, cold calling, sending out press releases, booking flights, negotiating fees, even buying flowers. Because it was such a small set up, if I'd make a mistake it could have had enormous consequences.'

Ursula knew that many other graduates would have loved this particular role, but although it gave her all sorts of skills, she quickly realised that she did not want to stay. 'It was poor pay and not even related to classical music, which was my big love.' She sat down and thought through all the jobs that she could do and all the abilities that she had. At the time, she had a boyfriend who was an architect and she was writing for his website. 'I got a kick out of producing well-worded persuasive copy even if I didn't have much idea about the technical realities. I picked up on themes – light, movement, ambience. I was writing instinctively.'

Ursula decided to try copy writing but had no idea how to get into that, so instead left her original job and took unpaid placements with a range of publishers – some good, some indifferent – and with a literary agent. 'I was fortunate to be able to afford to do that for a while. I wasn't short of work – I was teaching music in my spare time and also running an orchestra, playing in quartets and "fixing" ensemble performances. I was still a bit confused as to my direction and then a friend of a friend suggested applying for a job that he knew of with a telecoms company. It was as an editor, which meant I would skip several rungs on the publishing ladder, as well as having the sort of salary and corporate perks that you don't often get in mainstream publishing.

When I first started, I received excellent training, which eased me into editing texts I knew nothing about. But bit by bit I built up an understanding of the subject area. I've honed my editorial skills – for instance we even have meetings to discuss hyphenation – and I've gained a lot of professional confidence – I can now do PowerPoint presentations to colleagues and clients, for instance.

Ursula is now in something of a dilemma: 'I have to decide between the corporate environment and the arts environment. If I went back into the latter, I'd have to take a pay cut and learn new technical skills such as QuarkXPress or InDesign (publishing design packages). Mainstream editing is difficult unless you come from a wealthy family – the pay will always be low.'

The skills Ursula gained from her degree . . .

- Musical skills, including reading music scores at a high level – which she will always maintain.
- Analytical skills: 'in music of course, but I've transposed those to words'.
- Acute attention to detail: 'When reading music you have to have a very sharp eye for taking in detail in order to reproduce it quickly while playing.' Again, Ursula has used this in another context as an editor.
- Pedantry – which has proved hugely helpful now.

. . . and from university life in general

Building relationships with a wide circle of artistic and creative friends, some of whom she still works with in a musical setting.

Ursula's advice

'If you feel a yen to be a musician, do it, because otherwise you might always regret it. It's a good idea to go for it straight after university, because then, if things don't work out, you'll still have time to reconsider after two to three years.'

12 Performing Arts, Theatre Studies and Drama

OVERVIEW

How many different disciplines fall under this heading? Acting, dance of all kinds, choreography, physical theatre, circus arts, theatre production, play writing, stage management and technical areas such as sound and lighting are all key areas, plus the academic study of drama itself. Many people who study different branches of performing arts specialise in one pathway, e.g. dance, but keep an eye on what's happening in other sectors and subsectors such as musical theatre. They often collaborate with students from other degrees such as film and music. This gives them an eclectic array of talents, aside from personal qualities such as resilience and mental and bodily stamina. All these are necessary in a field where, even as a student, you are in an environment that is competitive and often physically and emotionally draining.

It is notoriously difficult to find sustained employment in acting, dance and other performance fields: the 'resting actor' is a stereotype that is all too real. Most drama schools will try to prepare students for this by emphasising that about 90% of the profession is unemployed at any one time.

Many performers are adept at finding new ways to deploy their creative gifts while they are between jobs – writing and producing plays or doing research for TV companies. Often these jobs are as insecure as their original profession, so sometimes they have to resort to other ways of finding cash: temporary clerical assignments, working front of house or the traditional waiting on tables and serving drinks in pubs and bars. Some eventually succumb to the lure of permanent 'money jobs', having realised that they may not make it professionally.

WHAT WILL YOU GAIN FROM STUDYING DRAMA, THEATRE STUDIES OR PERFORMING ARTS?

In any aspect of performance, you have to learn early on how to cope with rejection, disappointment and criticism, so this often bestows a great deal of self-awareness. Career-wise, this area has many parallels with music, and, to a lesser extent, with art and design, so take a look at these chapters for further enlightenment.

CAREER POSSIBILITIES

What can you do if you decide against treading the boards? Paul Kleiman of PALATINE, the Higher Education Academy's centre for supporting learning and teaching in dance, drama and music, points out that graduates from these courses have myriad 'soft' skills that employers could use: flexibility, an innovative and creative perspective, an aptitude for coping with uncertainty and taking on responsibility, a flair for communication and team work plus, in many cases, an entrepreneurial streak and problem-solving abilities. Our three case studies offer some clues as to where such qualities can be put to good use: none of them went into performance areas but they are all using the skills they learned to build satisfying careers elsewhere. In fact, if you want to hear about an actual actor, go straight to Chapter 3 where you'll find Jake Harders, a classics graduate, who worked as a management consultant before retraining at the Central School of Speech and Drama. He tells of the highs and lows of his way of life: success in his field may not bring large financial rewards, but it does seem to bring self-content!

GRADUATE DESTINATIONS

See Chapter 11 for an outline of the findings of HESA on destinations of performing arts graduates.

CASE STUDY

Name: David Swain
Job role: Administrator, Almieda Theatre
Qualifications: *Degree*: BA Drama (First), Goldsmiths College, University of London *A levels*: **Theatre studies, English Language and Literature** *BTEC National*: **Performing Arts**

Although David feels that he ended up at Goldsmiths by default – 'it was one of only two universities to offer me a place' – he certainly made the most of his time there. Overcoming the initial culture shock of leaving a fairly sheltered existence in his native Hull, he quickly settled into the degree.

'At first it was a jolt to the system and not what I was expecting. The Goldsmiths' emphasis was on post modern and avant garde drama and the onus was on us students to be creative and "out there". I wasn't used to that – I was originally interested in musical theatre! But I ended up devising new stuff and developing new interests.'

He took advantage of being in London by going to see as much drama as possible and also by becoming a part-time box office assistant in a well-known theatre five days a week. 'Every day, I'd cross Waterloo Bridge and go to the Lyceum for the start of my shift and I'd almost have to pinch myself that I was there in the heart of the West End. That chance to become familiar with how front of house operates was invaluable and I've been able to build on that ever since.'

Then suddenly David found himself nearing the end of his course, still fairly unsure of what was to follow. 'Some people went off to do postgrad acting courses, but although I'd done some performance as part of the course, that wasn't on my agenda. I had a few careers meetings, maybe a little late in the day, and decided that the main option was to pursue a career in theatre administration. I saw a relevant vacancy for the Orange Tree Theatre in Richmond and applied for it.' David freely admits that he did not even expect to get an interview – he knew that such an opportunity at a well-regarded 'off West End' theatre would be highly sought after. But luck was with him and he was taken on as a trainee.

David was eventually able to apply for a job share with another junior colleague at the Orange Tree, combining box office work with marketing and is eternally grateful that the theatre put its faith in two raw recruits, instead of taking on someone more experienced.

'It was a fulfilling role and the box office duties balanced it out and complemented it. Plus it was another thing to put on my CV.'

When another job arose at the Almeida, a prestigious 'off West End' venue in Islington, David threw his hat into the ring and was, once again, taken on. 'It meant going back to administration but at a bigger theatre with a higher turnover and a track record of innovative productions and transfers into mainstream houses. After two years, I'm now one of the most experienced members of staff there and my duties have expanded from entry level into all sorts of other avenues. Apart from doing some general management, I'm effectively a production assistant, as well as taking on some human resources duties, including sorting out work permits. I also arrange travel and accommodation for the artists. All this is combined with the more banal admin support that one always has to do, but it will all come in handy for the future.'

What does David see himself doing some years down the line? 'I'm not sure what my next move will be, but I'm sure I'll spot a likely opportunity when it comes up. It could be a sideways move – theatre doesn't always offer linear progression. Whatever it is, it will be the next step on the path to production or general management, though there may be other things that I would like to do as well. Few theatres offer such scope as somewhere like the Almeida; we have a reputation for quality. There are over 30 staff here and all sorts of possibilities may come up as people move on.'

The skills David gained from his degree . . .

He says, 'We didn't look at how theatres are run or aspects of production, though dramaturgy was touched on', so he doesn't think that his course gave him any core skills that he is using at the moment. However, his First Class Honours did help him stand out from the crowd when job hunting in an oversubscribed field.

. . . and from university life in general

'It helped me grow up, become independent, formulate opinions and see how the world works.'

David's advice

He points out that theatre administration is not a get rich quick occupation. Financially, 'I was probably better off as a student in some ways!' Nonetheless, for those who want to pursue this

dering TV instead. Ealing had a television studios in
ended up working as an unpaid runner there on a
y Labs for Channel 4.'

he managed to prove his worth, and after a few
noted to paid status. 'It was the lowest possible rate,
st a rate!' He was then recommended as a runner
duction team involved with a comedy series and has
ack. Work came in fairly regularly and Dan attributes
epeat work for small companies. 'I've never worked
Endemol or any of the big players yet.' This strategy
m make the leap from runner to junior researcher, then
'Some people are runners for maybe two years and
st about being a dogsbody. So I was very fortunate.'

int, Dan had worked on comedy shows only, but
ontract with Avalon for a piece they were delivering
was about comedy and comedians but was more of an
cumentary'. A few months into the contract he was
nt producer. 'It wasn't any more money, but it meant
put that on my CV and, from then on, I was regarded
t a researcher. I'd also stepped away from comedy,
ok for more scope with my next jobs. For example,
actual/reality stuff in the Caribbean and a historical
ry. I didn't have to show any knowledge of history – they
because they knew I could deliver.'

so worked on some children's TV and is currently working
y Belle Productions, which is involved in a cultural project
s. 'It's really exciting: Clive Anderson will be presenting and
g to feature artists such as Anthony Gormley.'

her year or so as AP, he will be ready to seek work as a
in his own right. Currently he is in the lucky position of
to negotiate good fees and believes that he is well paid
e is in employment. The freelance life is not without its
ks, however, and when the recession struck in 2008/9, Dan
at work was coming in more slowly, if at all. He had periods
ployment during which he took clerical jobs and, when
se started drying up, he had to register with more temping
s. He says more about the pros and cons of a freelance work
Chapter 1. Apart from these glitches, Dan can't envisage
in any other way. 'It's all I've ever known and I certainly
nagine being in one job for ever and ever!'

profession, David suggests being proactive and taking advantage of every opportunity. 'Write to theatres and just accumulate what background and knowledge you can: most theatres are on the lookout for good interns and even a week's experience will count in an area where you need to get ahead of the competition!'

CASE STUDY

Name: Katie Barker
Job role: Learning Mentor, secondary school, south-east England
Qualifications: *Degree*: BA Joint Honours Drama and Classical Literature and Civilisation (2.ii), University of Birmingham
A levels: Drama, Psychology, Classical Civilisation

'Looking back now, I think I might have enjoyed the course more if I'd done single honours drama. It was only myself and one other person taking this particular combination, which was a bit isolating and sometimes I didn't feel part of either department! Meeting deadlines was hard because I had work for two different courses and taking a joint degree meant that I didn't have enough time for the practical side of drama.' Despite all these setbacks, Katie continued with her course.

'We covered the theory and background of drama, but there were plenty of opportunities to do more "hands on" stuff. I couldn't take up as many of these as I would have wished because of the joint requirement, maybe just one option each term. This included playwriting, stage combat and physical theatre.'

When Katie graduated, she found herself in limbo – as many other university leavers do if they haven't already fixed on a career. 'I chose my degree because I liked those subjects at school and I hadn't really thought any further forward than that. I was a bit unsure what to do next, especially as I felt that my results weren't what I had hoped. So I stepped back for a while and found work in a shop, while I figured out what to do next. I had always known that I didn't want to act or be in the theatre in any other capacity. On the other hand, I didn't want to let go of drama entirely. The notion of teaching or something in education was always at the back of my mind, but I needed to test the water first.'

Katie checked out teaching in a very intrepid manner, taking herself off to South Africa for a month. 'I went with Travellers Worldwide as a volunteer. We were based in a primary school where myself and another graduate taught drama, and other group members covered subjects like PE. The school was in quite a well to do suburb, but we did have contact with pupils in poorer areas too.'

How did this experience impact on her next move? 'This helped me decide that I wanted to find out more about teaching. I knew by then that I wanted to work in the secondary sector, but I also realised that getting into a Drama PGCE is very difficult: there's little government funding and very few places, particularly if you have a 2.ii. So I decided to find a job, any job as long as it involved student contact, in a school.'

Katie became a learning mentor, initially supporting sixth formers with their coursework. 'Obviously I couldn't assist them too much if they were taking maths or science, but my A levels and degree were broad enough that I could offer advice about most arts and humanities subjects. You didn't need to be a graduate to apply for the post, but it does make the role easier.' Katie did so well that the school asked her to work with a more demanding caseload. 'I'm now mentoring Years 10 and 11 students who are having difficulty engaging with school. They may be on reduced timetables and they all need help with their GCSEs and with wider issues. I do a lot of work with individuals within small groups.'

Katie is now looking forward to applying for drama teacher training in a year's time. 'I know it's competitive, but I hope that this experience will give me a boost.'

The skills Katie gained from her degree . . .

- Confidence: 'I'm much less shy than I was.'
- Learning to interact with other people.

. . . and from university life in general

- 'I found out more about myself. I realised I was making myself live up to ridiculously high expectations and that's where the pressure came from.'
- Making compromises: 'My work was good, but I wanted it to be perfect, so I'd spend so much time striving for excellence that I'd hand in a first class essay late and have marks deducted. I've now got a more balanced attitude!'
- Perseverance: 'I stuck it out even when it wasn't going well and got through some difficult times.'

Katie's advice

'A degree is very different
things don't work out, seek
put yourself under too muc
time at university even if it

CASE STUDY

Name: Dan Grey
Job role: Freelance Assistant T
Qualifications: *Degree*: Drama
Birmingham *A levels*: Theatre St

'I held offers from Birmingham a
to do drama, but I preferred the
Midlands. The course was fine – a
What it couldn't do was train you
start and then you would need to
this in mind but after my A levels
degree. We all had to do some per
but you were able to steer away fro
all sorts of things – dance, costume
terms we looked at the background
periods in drama and international t
black influences, etc. That led indirec
was about black playwrights in New
dealt with race and gender issues.'

It wasn't all work and no play for Dan
ran their own open mike comedy night
acquired funding from the Arts Counci
a disused local railway station. He also
Festival as a director. By the time he gra
an actor's life was not for him. 'I realised
and I lacked a bit of confidence too. Plus
I could deal with the poverty that an act
to go into film. By now I was living in Lor
who worked at Ealing Studios. He got me
basically uncovered the fact that I wasn't
film – which is really a prerequisite to gett

suggested consi
those days and
series of Comed

Luckily for Dan,
weeks was pror
but it was at le
to another proc
never looked b
that to doing
for the BBC or
also helped hi
to researcher.
basically it's ju

Up to this po
then took a c
for ITV. This
'observed do
made assista
that I could
as an AP, no
so I could lo
I did some
documenta
took me or

Dan has al
with Libert
for Sky Ar
we're goin

After ano
producer
being abl
– when h
drawbac
found th
of unem
even the
agencie
style in
working
can't in

The skills Dan gained from his degree . . .

- Dan's degree was very project-based, which he feels was a good preparation for production – and many other types of jobs. 'We were constantly working in teams, coming up with ideas, getting these off the ground and making them happen'.
- He also learnt to work within a budget, 'which is important if you're in charge of any artistic activity'.
- The drama foundation was also useful when Dan first started in TV because he was working in a 'scripted' field: 'It was the same skills in a different arena: breaking down the script, looking for themes, putting what was needed into place.'

. . . and from university life in general

'I was very young and although I do know people who have gone into TV fresh out of school, it wouldn't have suited me. University got me ready for work.'

Dan's advice

'A degree is what you make it! So it's really up to you to get it working for you. As for TV, when I first began, I found it pretty daunting. I kept a low profile and knuckled down to some hard work. I saw how the hierarchy operated and what I had to do to move forward. Confidence comes with experience.'

13 Philosophy

OVERVIEW

Emma Gordon, our first case study, was at pains to bolster the image of the subject. *'It's not all about Greek and Roman blokes in togas making wishy washy arguments,'* she says. Read on if you want to find out more about philosophy's applicability to modern life and some perhaps unexpected career choices.

WHAT WILL YOU GAIN FROM STUDYING PHILOSOPHY?

The skills you will gain by reading philosophy are the same as those gained by other arts graduates – with perhaps even more emphasis on logical reasoning, since most philosophy students study logic as an integral part of the course. This leads a significant number into careers as computer programmers and analysts. They can also understand complex arguments, produce their own conclusions – once again in an area where there are no correct answers – and give the evidence necessary to support their opinions. They can solve problems, express ideas and communicate both orally and in writing.

CAREER POSSIBILITIES

There is only one career that this subject leads to directly, and that is teaching (or more likely lecturing in higher education, since, although the subject does exist at A level, it is not taught in many schools). Philosophy graduates still enter a varied range of careers, however. (See Introduction for examples in addition to those given here.) In particular, philosophy can lead to the following careers: computing, information management, information science, information technology, insurance claims assessing, insurance underwriting, law – barrister or solicitor and publishing – editing, proofreading.

GRADUATE DESTINATIONS

'What do graduates do?' does not cover philosophy, but destination figures across several universities show philosophy graduates working in areas such as those listed above plus advertising, banking, management consultancy, marketing, self-employed arts consultant, social work, teaching English as a foreign language, youth work and film directing.

CASE STUDY

Name: Emma Gordon
Job role: PhD Student and Undergraduate Tutor, Edinburgh University
Qualifications: *Degrees*: MA Philosophy (First), University of Glasgow; Taught MA in Philosophy at the University of Edinburgh, currently working towards a PhD in Philosophy at the same university *Advanced Highers*: Music, English, Religious, Moral and Philosophical Studies

'I started off on a psychology degree but it really wasn't what I expected and my lack of a science background was a drawback. In the first year, the course also included sociology and philosophy and I quickly realised that this was where my interests lay and switched. I was very happy with my choice: it covered all the elements that I'd enjoyed before university and meshed with my interests. A lot of people have the wrong impression about philosophy – it's very contemporary. We were looking at morality, at ethics, what was morally acceptable across the board. For instance, we covered environmental issues, animal rights, criminal justice.'

The system in Scotland meant that Emma's first degree lasted a whole four years and was an MA rather than a BA. By the time she reached her final year she knew which way she hoped her career might go. She wanted to teach her subject and preferred to do that in the higher education system. ('I just didn't think that I was personally suited to working in a school with teenagers.') This meant that she would have to go on to further study – first a master's, then a PhD, also known as a doctorate. She successfully applied to Edinburgh for the master's programme in philosophy. Unlike some masters' courses, formal research methods were not taught as a separate subject, but Emma doesn't see this as a drawback. 'Everyone is friendly and we all help each other and talk about what research we're doing and how to tackle it.'

In order to move on to the doctorate, Emma had to submit a research proposal. 'This was needed because of the great competition for funding. I found it quite stressful. You have about 250 words in which to market yourself, which isn't easy. Fortunately I had great support from my supervisor.'

The field of philosophy that Emma chose to follow was epistemology, the study of knowledge itself, in particular its origins, breadth and validity. Part of what she is doing is comparing knowledge to understanding. Her thesis is provisionally titled 'Epistemic value, epistemic luck and sceptism'. 'It's the area of philosophy which I find most fascinating. My research is working out well and I can fully devote my time to what I care about. The department has a lively atmosphere and everyone discusses their work. There's a huge amount of reading to do, both books and scholarly papers.'

This is just one aspect of Emma's time at the university. The other side is the teaching duties, which she undertakes with first-year undergraduates: 'I tutor two groups of 20–30 first year philosophy students, just dealing with the fundamentals of the subject. It was intimidating at first as I'd had no training, but all the PhD students were in the same boat so we traded tips and ideas and learned as a group. We have suggested to the university that more training and assessment would be a good idea for the future and, who knows, it might mean more pay!'

In addition, Emma marks course work essays (30 of them, three times a year) and exam essays too (30 again, twice a year). 'Again, we received no training for this but all the tutors met during the first marking session in order to moderate our marks and check that we were being fair. Marking course work is a lot easier than marking exams, given the incoherence of most first-year students under pressure and issues involving bad handwriting! We tend to mark less harshly when going over exam essays. When it comes to course work, as well as giving my students their grades I give them a sheet of comments – we're not obligated to do this, but I know I found it helpful when tutors did this for me as an undergraduate. On the comment sheet, I indicate things that were done well, which the student should try to replicate in other essays, and (tactfully) point out areas the students could improve on/flaws in their arguments.'

What happens after the PhD is completed? Some students go on to do postdoctoral research, but Emma would prefer not to just concentrate on this. 'I want to go on lecturing because I really enjoy it. That's not to say that if a good post-doc opportunity came up I wouldn't take it. I'm also prepared to go anywhere in the world – as other former colleagues have done.'

The skills Emma gained from her degree . . .

- Problem solving – 'which I can apply on a day-to-day basis as well as academically.'
- Evaluating and structuring an argument.
- Being able to take a more balanced view when assessing other people's views: 'I'm much less emotional, much less dogmatic.'
- 'Something else I've gained from postgraduate study is the opportunity to go abroad to present papers at conferences. Quite often, the department will fund postgrad students to do this, too, paying for flights and accommodation. Conferences are a great way to network in your field, learn about exciting new research and see new parts of the world at the same time.'

. . . and from university life in general

Emma feels that she got more out of her further degrees than her undergraduate programme. 'I met more like-minded people at postgraduate level, so there was more opportunity for rigorous discussion. I felt on my first degree that a few people had just fallen into it and weren't always prepared to work hard.'

Emma's advice

'If you're thinking about a PhD, work on your proposal and apply for funding as early as possible because it's a stringent process. Some people do manage without scholarships, awards and bursaries, but it's a lot easier if you have these in place. Look hard at which universities will best support your research and develop your interests – not all departments are the same. You can study all kinds of specialist areas at this level – for instance feminist philosophy. That would have left me all at sea but it's worth taking time to find out what's out there.'

CAREER NOTE

For most full-time permanent university teaching posts it is necessary to have at least a master's degree. However, it is more usual to take a PhD if you want to make a serious career in academia and become a full-time lecturer. This could involve another three or four years of study and your research must be in an original topic – one not already covered by other scholars – hence the importance of writing a finely tuned initial proposal. Most PhD students teach or demonstrate to undergraduates as part of their duties. It's also important to write papers and have these published, to attend and present at conferences and to get yourself known in your discipline.

Funding is always an issue, not just at PhD stage but also when trying to secure money for departmental research and other activities, so Emma's experience of applying for a scholarship will come in handy later on.

CASE STUDY

Name: Gareth Barker
Job role: Assistant Brand Manager, Procter & Gamble
Qualifications: *Degree*: BA Philosophy and Literature (2.i), Warwick University *A levels*: English Literature, History, Religious Studies

Gareth first became interested in philosophy when he studied it as part of his religious studies A level: 'That really whetted my appetite for more and the course at Warwick was fantastic – one of the few degrees that really integrated the two subjects that interested me. Apart from the core modules, we were able to take lots of optional subjects. I did German just to improve my language skills and also creative writing – which allowed me to write poetry – alongside more traditional philosophical elements such as formal logic. That was horrendous: it involved putting sentences into algebraic formula! There was also a huge amount of reading to do – two or three books per week.'

Gareth loved his degree but had given no real thought to careers. He worked part-time in the students' union and, as a result, in his third year his thoughts were very focused on standing for student union office and hence having a paid sabbatical for a fourth year at university. 'For that fourth year I was Communications Development Officer. It was all about improving ENTS (the entertainment offered) and bars and restaurant facilities. I don't think I'd have got my current job if it hadn't have been for that.'

But Gareth still hadn't quite found his career niche, applying mainly for graduate schemes in central and local government, getting to the final stages of each selection post before falling at the final hurdle. 'The problem was that I had no real passion for what I was applying for. When I was tested at interview as to why I wanted the job, I couldn't really explain. My application to Procter & Gamble came about by chance. A friend working there suggested it. I already knew a little bit about marketing from my sabbatical role in the Students' Union, and when I looked further into the role I decided it was perfect for me.'

When Gareth got the job, he found that his first few weeks in post were a baptism of fire. 'Procter & Gamble have no graduate scheme as such – you get a "real" job with total responsibility for your brand from the very beginning. I was sent to Dublin and was looking after the Pampers and feminine care brands across the whole of Ireland. I had a budget and had to decide on promotion, marketing and communications strategies.'

Gareth survived and thrived and is now back in the UK, heading the brand operations for Gillette, Braun and Oral B. Again he is in charge of a budget and has to plan how to maximise it for TV, print, radio and internet exposure, as well as looking after local sports marketing. 'Some of the things that I have covered over the last four years are new product launches, media planning, communication and promotion strategy development, and general business management. I particularly enjoy working with different agencies – planning and buying, digital, creative – and developing launch plans for brands such as Gillette, Braun and Oral B. It's fun, it's creative and you can actually see the results in the marketplace.'

The skills Gareth gained from his degree . . .

- Analysis and logical thinking.
- Learning how to write well and how to structure an argument.
- The ability – which, as he points out, is transferable – 'to take huge amounts of information and to prioritise and synthesise it down to what's most important. If you are reading several 800-word books a week, that's a must.'

. . . and from university life in general

- Time management.
- The leadership skills that came from his sabbatical year, and involvement in the Rugby club (discussed in more detail on Chapter 2).

Gareth's advice

See Chapter 2 for a fuller version of Gareth's advice, the nub of which is that getting a strong result in your degree is important, but perhaps more significant in today's competitive jobs market is to add depth to your CV by taking active leadership roles in a breadth of extra-curricular activities. Companies such as Proctor & Gamble look for this as much as academic success.

CASE STUDY

Name: Philip Bassot
Job role: Graduate Trainee in Advertising, Kameleon
Qualifications: *Degree*: BA Cultural Studies (2.i), Leeds University; Advanced Professional Diploma in Advertising, West Herts College
A levels: Maths, Economics, Art

For Philip, it was always a dilemma whether to go for arts subjects or indulge his love of maths and related areas. Like many undergraduates, he made one false start, beginning a fashion foundation course before deciding it wasn't for him.

'I absolutely loved the Leeds degree – it was amazing, although I think that the university seriously undersold it. There was a heavy drop-out rate initially, because some people felt that it wasn't what they'd signed up for, but it really grabbed me once I got into it. We started off by studying Marx, then went on to Foucault and Nietchsze, and we also covered linguistics, aesthetics and history of art along the route. It was all done in a holistic way – for instance how linguistics impacted on psycho-analysis and how they both influenced art. The over-arching theme was philosophy, which I studied a little before, but it seemed very dry compared with what we were doing. This was culturally relevant – we were really following movements in philosophy and their effect on all aspects of 20th-century life. I loved looking at familiar concepts from new angles. We could pretty much do what we liked with assignments: tutors would suggest themes but you could write about what interested you – as long as it was relevant.'

In his second year, Phil started writing for the university newspaper and ended up co-editing the fashion section. 'I was always torn between journalism and advertising, but when the time came to decide on postgrad study, one of the things that swayed me was the course fees. The diploma in advertising that I took was a lot cheaper than doing a master's in journalism!'

The course was at West Herts College in Watford, which offers mainly further education rather than higher-level studies, but is well established as a training ground for those who want to go into the advertising industry. Philip has a bit of a salutary tale to tell here . . .

'The website was confusing and I actually ended up on the wrong course by mistake! There were two possibilities: one for would-be creatives such as copywriters and art directors and one that looked at the wider area of advertising. I had hoped to go on the copywriting diploma, so I was initially disappointed to find myself on the more general course.' This could have been disastrous, and it certainly illustrates the importance of reading the small print, but the tale has a happy ending. 'I really warmed to what I was doing and realised that I didn't want to be confined to such a narrow field. It turned out that I was more interested in planning and strategy. There was a creative element that I enjoyed, but the profession is evolving rapidly as we enter the digital era, and we came away with portfolios that were very marketable to smaller innovative agencies.'

Philip particularly appreciated the chance to get to grips with live assignments, making real 'pitches' for major products to actual agencies. 'But the best part was the work experience, which we were encouraged to seek out for ourselves. My first placement was in a more traditional agency, my second in a start-up business called Kameleon and my third came right at the end of the diploma. As regards jobs, I applied to lots of the better-known graduate schemes with very little success, but on my last day at West Herts, Kameleon asked me to come on board. It's just a team of five, getting involved in all sorts of cutting-edge projects – more sponsorship-based than traditional advertising. We're doing something with Vodafone that will see online drama content sent straight to people's mobiles.'

It's early days yet, but Philip is very excited about the future. 'The salary is not fantastic, but with bonuses I should be making as much as people who have gone onto the bigger schemes. My placement gave me a good idea of what to expect. We are so small that it means getting involved with everything – research, contributing ideas and brainstorming, account planning. If I find out that I want to specialise in – say, the strategy side – I'll be able to tailor my job spec to this and grow with the company. I loved my degree and wanted to be doing a job that I also loved – I've been very fortunate.'

The skills Philip gained from his degree . . .

- 'It really changed the way I thought. Getting to know more about logic and reasoning has altered the way I argue a case.'
- 'I'm more aware of the use of language and how messages are open to different interpretations.'
- 'Learning a new way of approaching academic subjects: unlike maths there is often not a right answer!'

. . . and from university life in general

Just making fantastic friends: 'the people were brill!'

Philip's advice

'I wish I'd thought about more about my career while I was at university: for instance, I shouldn't have spent all my summers travelling, when some internships would have been useful instead. I loved my degree and wanted to do a job I loved too, but, career-wise, an arts qualification involves luck and something extra to complement the degree. I'd certainly recommend getting involved with something outside the course – I fell into editing and this was great experience that didn't feel like work.'

14 Religious Studies and Theology

OVERVIEW

Whatever the popular view of religious studies and theology, they are broad and academically testing subjects. They are not merely about studying the Bible, the Koran or other holy books and literature. Nor do they usually focus exclusively on one faith: even if they are, for instance, nominally about Christian or Jewish ideology, they need to take into account other views and religions.

Do these courses appeal only to those with firmly held beliefs? Not necessarily. Josh Warren, our first case study, approached his degree in a spirit of intellectual curiosity, while Andy Bishop notes that his subject attracted a variety of believers, non-believers and doubters. Some courses do have a reputation for attracting those with a strong religious faith, so it's wise to find out what the underlying ethos of the degree is before committing yourself to three or four years of study. In a nutshell, do you want to be with like-minded people and foster your own religious development or would you prefer to have access to a variety of ideas, cultures and viewpoints?

WHAT WILL YOU GAIN FROM STUDYING RELIGIOUS STUDIES AND THEOLOGY?

Most courses demand a willingness to engage objectively with difficult and sensitive issues, with a range of (sometimes conflicting) beliefs and with ideas that have a contemporary resonance although they may be centuries old. They require an ability to learn from others, to probe, to explore, to analyse, unpick and to propound and follow closely reasoned arguments. They also involve an understanding of philosophy, logic, ancient and modern history, sociological issues and, often, some knowledge of archaeology and archaic languages to boot! All in all, extremely well rounded and multi-faceted! Graduates in these disciplines are highly marketable to a variety of employers across many professions.

CAREER POSSIBILITIES

Many graduates of theology and religious studies do go on to study for some kind of religious ministry, but there are numerous alternative routes. Those who enjoy the academic and intellectual side of these subjects can pursue this further through relevant master's and PhD studies. At the moment, postgraduate courses covering areas such as peace studies are popular ways of continuing to engage with theological and religious issues on a wider plane.

For those who decide to enter employment, careers with a pastoral element are popular, e.g. youth work, social work, teaching, human rights, charities and international development. Beyond this, there is infinite potential to follow other interests: for instance, two of Josh Warren's classmates are currently working in human resources and in web design.

GRADUATE DESTINATIONS

'What do graduates do?' does not refer to these subjects, but used as 'a degree of any discipline', graduates in these fields can hold their own against all comers.

CASE STUDY

Name: Josh Warren
Job role: Teacher, inner London comprehensive school
Qualifications: *Degree*: BA Study of Religions (First), School of Oriental and African Studies (SOAS), University of London, followed by a Postgraduate Certificate in Education (PGCE) *A levels*: Sociology, Psychology, Religious Studies

Josh was just about to take up his first teaching post when he contributed this profile. He says that he took religious studies (RS) on a whim at A level and had no career in mind at that point – except that he knew for sure that he didn't want to teach.

'When I was applying to university I looked for a degree that would sustain my interest for three or four years. I really enjoyed my RS A level and grew particularly interested in Buddhism, so I picked SOAS for the diversity of its course content and its student body. The modular nature of the course meant that we could focus on specific areas of the world and the growth of faiths within these – for instance Asia, Buddhism and philosophy of religion, Africa and anthropology. We were also able to take relevant languages – I studied Japanese in my third year. My classmates came from all over the world, often to study their own religions, and many of them were mature. So it perhaps made for a slightly different experience than the average undergraduate degree.'

Josh found his time at SOAS fascinating. He did not come from a religious background, but was interested to find out what motivated religious belief and how it had affected history and society. But by his third year he was no closer to having a career plan – apart from wavering in his refusal to contemplate teaching: 'I knew I wanted to stay with my subject and I considered academia but, having investigated it, I felt that for me it would be too narrow – and likely to become narrower as time went on.'

So during his final months at SOAS, Josh did some voluntary work with young people who had special needs as a means of developing his confidence in working with youngsters and perhaps moving into teaching. He also attended an open schools event where potential PGCE students could spend a day in school. He says of this catalyst, 'I realised that actually I didn't mind being in a classroom with grumpy teenagers!'

Nonetheless, he was disinclined to spend another year in full-time study so soon after his degree, so found work as a teaching assistant in a London prep school. 'I did some admin, helped out in the classroom, supervised the children in the playground and the canteen and went on some residential trips. I also managed to hook up with the RE department and delivered a couple of "proper" lessons.'

The whole experience made Josh come to terms with what he did and didn't want. He decided against teaching in private education but 'I figured out where I wanted to be. I found out about working in the state school system by talking to student teachers and those already in the profession. I went in to the PGCE with my eyes wide open.'

Josh found the course to be vocational with elements of master's-level study thrown in. 'You're not really a student – you have to be a professional: it's a different set of skills. It was much more work than my BA. Some people say it's the toughest year of your life! Others think that that's your NQT (Newly Qualified Teacher) year, which I guess I'm just about to find out.'

He thinks that he developed very quickly through his first school placement. 'I had a good mentor there, which can be a matter of luck, and everyone on the course was well supported by tutors and mentors. But you've either got the confidence and the experience before you start or not and just being in a classroom helps you find your feet.'

Having spent time in two very different inner city schools, Josh is well prepared for his first teaching post. 'One of my schools was just shifting in terms of demographics and having to take in a broader social mix, the other was Afro Caribbean/Middle Eastern/European heritage, so you discover how to deal with different cultural and educational sensitivities. Where I'll be working now is different again – we have a lot of Bengali pupils.'

He counts himself as very lucky. 'This was the first job I applied for and my first real interview.' Many of his PGCE year have not yet found jobs. How is he feeling about his new post? 'Many schools now concentrate on cross-curricular themes, with perhaps less need for specialisation and in that sense you might need to adapt your teaching style. In my case, I'm in a faith school so the emphasis will be on RE. The syllabus is heavy on both Christianity and Islam – not my areas of expertise, so that will test my own learning and knowledge.'

The skills Josh gained from his degree . . .

- 'It gave me empathy, understanding, cross-cultural awareness and really awareness of the world itself.'
- 'It opened my mind too. The lecturers at SOAS were brilliant and really helped me to look at everything from a new perspective.'

. . . and from university life in general

'There is minimal teaching time and a huge book list, so it's up to you to develop your ability to pursue your own interests, while fulfilling the criteria for the course, naturally!'

Josh's advice

'If you take the PGCE, be aware that it is academic as well as skills-based. Many of my classmates were excellent on a practical basis, but found it difficult to adjust to the high level of research and study that was needed.'

CAREER NOTE

To teach pupils aged 4–16 in the state education system in the
UK, it is necessary to gain Qualified Teacher Status (QTS).
The most popular way of doing this is through the PGCE
course on a full-time or part-time basis, though there are
alternatives, which involve training on the job while studying.
The website of the Training and Development Agency for
Schools has comprehensive information on all aspects of a
career in teaching (www.tda.gov.uk).

CASE STUDY

Name: Andy Bishop
Job role: Inner-city Probation Officer/Offender Manager
Qualifications: *Degree*: BA Theology and Philosophy (2.i), University of
Birmingham *A levels*: English Literature, Sports Studies, Communication
Studies

Andy is another one of our case studies who had a slight hiccup
after A levels. He started a sports science degree but quickly realised
it wasn't for him, and took some time out before starting afresh
at Birmingham. The course was split 50/50 between the two joint
honours subjects, which Andy found worked well together.

'It was a good combination: they informed each other. Perhaps the
theology department was more forward looking than philosophy at
that time. It had a fresh, new approach and we studied topics such
as gay theology and black theology, which were a departure from
tradition. Although the course was based around Christian theology,
the ethos was academic rather than religious. You didn't need to be
a committed Christian to enjoy it: I suspect that there were atheists
and agnostics amongst both students and staff. A lot if it was about
discussing contemporary themes – had clubbing or following sports
teams replaced God, for instance.'

It was not until his third year that Andy began thinking about
the future. Like many arts graduates he'd taken his degree out of
interest, rather than to progress a career idea. 'I knew I wanted
something people-related. I'd done a fair amount of youth work
before and during my degree, but had become a little disillusioned
with the lack of structure and certain other aspects of the job. We
had a family friend who was quite senior in the probation service and

I talked to him before deciding. I liked the idea of clear boundaries around what you were doing.'

Andy made his application while doing finals. 'I think the theology was a help at interview. It was seen as a positive because it enabled me to argue and analyse.'

In his current role, Andy says that he really doesn't know what the day will hold until he gets to the office. His team has a caseload split between those in custody and those in the community. 'I think people have an image of probation officers being like social workers but we're really part of the law enforcement service.'

Naturally the job entails some degree of crisis management as the unexpected can and does happen, but Andy and his colleagues try to prepare for this by being as organised as possible. 'For our clients in custody we do sentence planning and regular reviews. It does involve visiting prisons as well as being desk-based. Our parole clients need help with benefits, healthcare, finding work and training. There's a lot of liaison with other agencies such as the police and social services to put together a risk assessment plan. We can recall anyone who re-offends or who breaks the terms of their probation.'

What tips would he give to those thinking of going into the probation service? He suggests getting some relevant work experience before deciding. 'You don't necessarily have to have a specific background in working with offenders or ex-offenders. But it's important to have some understanding of how to support people in difficulty and those who are vulnerable.'

The skills Andy gained from his degree . . .

'It has helped me to be able to unpick issues, which is a great asset when it comes to analysing case summaries and offences. In this role, it's important not to make assumptions, to read between the lines and to dig deep: I learnt all those skills on my course and also how to take part in discussions and debates without becoming aggressive.'

Andy's advice

'Theology degrees vary depending on where you study. Have a look at the course content, not just the title. Find out if the focus is academic or religious, Christian or mixed faith. Those with a strong belief may expect a religious base. Ask yourself why you have picked this subject and what you want to get out of it.'

15 Careers Advice and Job Hunting

FREQUENTLY ASKED QUESTIONS

All sorts of urban myths and half-truths surround careers provision in universities. Before hearing from some careers advisers and employers, let's distinguish fact from fiction.

Q: Can I only visit the careers service if I know what I want to do?

A: If you have an idea about what profession(s) you want to enter, you can use the careers centre to access further information and to discuss applications and interviews. But it's certainly not mandatory to have even an inkling about your next move before crossing the careers service threshold. Part of a careers adviser's role is to help people become more self-aware and able to choose realistic options. It can be a long drawn out process, not a one-off discussion, so to wait until you have a definitive career idea would be massively unproductive.

Q: Does the careers service give priority to final year students and those about to complete postgraduate courses?

A: In some universities, the careers centre may contact students who are about to leave to remind them of the resources available, but they are highly unlikely to turn other deserving cases away. There is usually a policy of first come, first served. You are welcome to use the service from your first day as an undergraduate and are encouraged to start your career planning as early as possible.

Q: Do you have to pay to use the careers service?

A: While you are studying, access to the careers service is free – you have paid for this sort of support indirectly through your fees, so use it! Don't let it be like the gym subscription that goes to waste. Once you leave your first or subsequent degree courses, different universities operate a variety of systems. Some will allow alumni to use the service for free for a limited number of years, others will make a small charge. Best to find out about this *before* you graduate.

Remember that if you do defer any careers investigations until after you complete your degree, you could miss out on the full range of help available and, just as importantly, you may find that deadlines for applying to major employers have passed.

Q: Will the careers service get you a job when you graduate?

A: Very few services will match individual students to job opportunities. But most of them have vacancy databases containing permanent and temporary jobs, plus voluntary work and internships. It is up to you to keep an eye on these and to sign up for any optional extras: for instance, many careers centres will notify students by email or text if opportunities come up in areas in which they have registered an interest.

Q: Does the careers service bring employers in to give talks and interview students for jobs?

A: This varies from university to university. The days of the extended 'milk round' (when recruiters visited numerous campuses in turn to see potential candidates) are long gone. Most careers services will have good employer links and will invite them to a range of events such as fairs and seminars. They may also draft them in to help with other activities such as workshops on, for example, negotiation techniques or team building. However, much recruitment is now done centrally – typically over the web. What the careers centre can do is signpost you to the most reliable sources of employer information and help you to use it to maximum advantage.

Specialist institutions such as drama schools and art colleges will also promote termly events and end of year showcases to employers and agents – or ask student to do so themselves.

Departmental tutors may have good contacts with employers and arrange for them to drop by. They might also hear of vacancies and internships. So keep your ear to the ground while you are still studying and stay in touch with your lecturers when you leave.

Q: Is the careers service any good for students who haven't the time or resources to visit it?

A: If you're studying on a remote site or on a part-time basis or you're simply too busy with your studies, some careers centres are open one evening a week. They will also try, whenever possible, to come into departments to give seminars or hold individual meetings with students. Many careers services have championed career planning modules, which students can opt into as an accredited part of the course or as a voluntary activity. The other possibility for long-distance communication with your careers service is, of course, via phone and email. E-guidance is now firmly established as one way of delivering careers help to students and graduates: it is often very effective, although it does have some obvious limitations.

Some well-established external organisations such as Prospects also offer guidance via email and through chatrooms. They may restrict this to those who have already graduated and could charge a small fee for some services.

WHAT DOES THIS MEAN FOR YOU WHILST AT UNIVERSITY AND BEYOND?

Before you can apply for a job you have to know what you want to do – not a decision that is often, or easily, made overnight. Your university careers advisory service can help you to come to a decision. They know a great deal about different careers – and employers – and what skills and subjects are required in different jobs. Note the phrase 'help you to come to a decision'. Students are often disappointed to find that a careers adviser cannot sprinkle some fairy dust and magic up an ideal job. The process involves students themselves doing quite a lot of work. The logical steps in choosing a career are:

- self-analysis: being aware of your skills, strengths, weaknesses, values and preferences
- occupational awareness: knowing what is involved in different jobs
- making choices
- applying.

Careers service staff can guide you through all of the above stages. When, then, should you make contact with your careers advisory service? As early as possible! You are highly unlikely to end freshers' week thinking, 'OK, now I'll make that careers appointment', but the sooner you do so the more help the service can give.

CAREER NOTE: NETWORKING

Before you read on, be aware that the term 'networking' will be mentioned several times in this chapter. It's an important tool in your job hunting repertoire, but not everyone understands how it functions or utilises it properly. You will probably use your careers service and other university careers websites to look for work. You'll scan the press and perhaps sign up with a few agencies as well. But if you omit to network, you could find yourself falling behind in the race to secure your goal. Networking is the art of using contacts – family, friends, acquaintances, neighbours – to be alert on your behalf. You've probably used it as a student when looking for accommodation. In careers terms, it could involve finding out if they know anyone who works in a field that interests you and then contacting that person for help and advice – not asking for a job, but perhaps requesting their time or support, or seeing if they can help with a placement.

You may not hit pay dirt with the first contact you make – it could be two or three people further down the line, but it's a tried and tested way of getting in and on, particularly in the arts and media. It has been proven to work in many other areas as well – law and stockbroking to name but two!

More formal networking can be done at employer events while still at university. Chat with the representatives rather than just concentrating on the cheese and wine, take away relevant business cards and follow through with a call or email within a week or so. Becoming a member of a professional body, such as the Chartered Society of Designers, Women in Publishing, and Incorporated Society of Musicians is another good tactic. These organisations will often lay on activities for the express purpose of socialising, learning more about your subject and – naturally – networking.

THE CAREERS ADVISER'S PERSPECTIVE

Fiona Thurley, The Careers Group, University of London

The Careers Group, University of London, is probably the UK's largest higher education careers service. It's the umbrella organisation that covers most of the constituent colleges belonging to London University, plus a number of other institutions. Fiona Thurley is one of 40+ careers advisers there. Her caseload, past and present, includes undergraduates and graduates from all disciplines, including all of the areas that we have looked at in this book. She herself took a classics degree, worked as a personal assistant and then in human resources, before training in her current role.

She stresses the importance of visiting your own careers service early. *'First year is fine. Certainly try not to leave it till you're just about to graduate as you may have missed out on all sorts of possibilities. The key thing is to do research your options, find out who you are and what you want and then take advantage of all the resources that the careers centre can offer.'*

Fiona explains all the additional facilities that a big service like The Careers Group can provide: *'We have college-based careers fairs throughout the year as well as at least three big central events annually. These attract students and graduates from all over the country. Autumn is our busiest time for employer presentations and we also have a programme of one and two day courses which are open to our own students – and often to those of other universities.'*

These have titles such as 'Start Your Own Business', 'Getting Into International Development' 'Arts Administration' 'Working In Charities', 'Work In the Media', 'The City Course' . . . it's a long list. Fiona is quick to stress that these are not merely 'chalk and talk'. *They're a real chance to get to know employers, chat with like-minded students, swap experiences and hear what it's really like from the horse's mouth. We make them interactive – we're keen that course members try out typical tasks and activities so that they can get a real flavour of what the work might entail.'*

Fiona's advice

'It's not necessarily more difficult for arts graduates to find jobs, as long as they are pro-active, but it may be less straightforward to figure out what they want to do. Perhaps they need to start earlier and work just that bit harder to get on track.'

Looking back to her own time at university, Fiona can see that she was the type of student who kept her head down and didn't really think about careers until she left. From her current perspective that may not be the ideal. *'You really do need to get involved – in societies in internships, in any form of work experience, paid or unpaid. Do something as well as your degree!'*

Julia Yates and Elaine Banham, the University of the Arts Careers Service, London

The University of the Arts London is made up of Camberwell College of Arts, Chelsea College of Art and Design, Central Saint Martin's, London College of Fashion, London College of Communications and Wimbledon College of Art. Julia Yates and Elaine Banham – joint Heads of Creative Careers there – explain what is different about careers work with their clients.

'*We think the key thing is that, even though the majority of our students are taking degrees which relate to specific practical skills, they don't necessarily have clearer career choices. It's almost as if the more specialised they are, the more specialist they're expected to become. For instance, a graphic designer would have to ask themselves, "Do I intend to work in print, corporate ID, brand, in 3D or moving image – or all these?", "Do I want to work in-house or freelance?" and all sorts of other questions around how they want to work. I suppose we're talking lifestyle choices – they need to consider a way of living that goes with a particular job.'*

Julia thinks that people who are trained in the creative disciplines have 'fantastic transferable skills' like project management or team working skills, which are less recognised compared to graduates from other sectors. *'We try to help our clients become opportunity aware and part of that is identifying their skills and knowing where else they can take these.'*

She also believes that although all graduate job hunting is competitive, it's particularly tough in the visual and performing arts. In addition, it is imperative to be imaginative in the way that the students approach job hunting. Elaine adds, *'We developed a unique advice and guidance tool with the CLIP CETL and Centre for Learning and Teaching (CLTAD) called Creative Living, which is designed to support art and design graduates in finding their way towards their goals in the creative industries.'*

In the University of the Arts London careers service, Creative Careers, Julia and Elaine's colleagues offer the traditional interviews, drop-in advice slots, panel discussions, industry visits and seminars, but above that, they spend time with students developing their transition skills and confidence. *'The career decision-making process is the same as for any group of graduates, but a lot of the workshops we do here are motivational and about building confidence – this is very important in a competitive environment,'* says Elaine. *'It's also about helping them develop a creative CV which stands out and communicates well within their area of the industry. Careers in art, crafts and design are less delineated and structured than those in mainstream employment so we provide a wealth of case study material, industry interviews and rely on productive collaborations with other university groups like the Alumni Association.'*

Creative Careers at the University of the Arts London also has access to other sources of advice and information such as the Enterprise Centre for the Creative Arts (ECCA) and Artquest, both of which are linked to the university but can also support graduates from this and other universities on a long-term basis.

Julia's advice

Although all graduate job hunting is competitive, it's particularly tough in the visual and performing arts. In addition, Julia feels that there is an imperative to be imaginative in the way that they approach job hunting. *'Many jobs are not actually advertised – so you might need to work for free to start with and you'll certainly have to try new strategies when looking for work. Networking is vital.'*

That's the view from two large careers services in London but there is a great deal of innovative careers provision throughout the country and it is certainly not confined to bigger universities.

Esyllt George, University of Wales Institute, Cardiff

The issues of employability and careers management skills are central to most higher education organisations. Employability is about giving students and graduates the skills outlined in Chapter 2 and helping them to apply these to the world of work.

Career management skills should enable graduates to make the transition from student to professional and then find the direction and way of working that suits them and meshes with their personal concept of 'success' (whether that means earning vast amounts of money, giving something back to society, maintaining a work–life balance or moving between jobs and career areas.)

The University of Wales Institute Cardiff (UWIC) serves an eclectic mix of students and courses, many of them arts-based, in the Welsh capital. Esyllt George, one of UWIC's small team of careers advisers, specialises in working with visual arts and humanities students.

'Many visual arts students look at ways of combining developing their art practice professionally while

simultaneously working in other jobs alongside this. It is part of my role to talk through the type of career and life structures that would suit an individual student best, and relate this to short- and long-term goals.'

How does Esyllt get to know her clients and at what stage in their university career does this happen? *'I try to introduce myself to students early in the first year so that they are aware of the careers service and how we respond to a range of needs, from in-depth guidance to specific information queries to practice interviews. Developing work experience, voluntary work and networking links with people outside the university can be very important. In the arts, many jobs are not advertised and effective networking can be a key to success. My careers education programme involves inviting a range of external professionals to meet and talk to the students. From these contacts some students are able to develop paid and voluntary work opportunities as well as broadening their awareness of different career options.'*

UWIC uses a virtual learning environment (VLE) to assist students with self-analysis and personal and professional development. *'We have developed a web-based blackboard career module for flexible student use to encourage self-awareness and self-reflection, with specific resources for arts students. We try to use a multi-faceted and creative approach to meet the needs of such a diverse mix of students on an increasingly wide range of arts courses.'*

Esyllt's advice

'Career decision making is an ongoing process of reflection and goal setting regarding an individual's pathway through life. For many arts students in particular, this can be a highly complex but exciting process of becoming self-aware and identifying a very wide range of possibilities.'

THE EMPLOYER'S PERSPECTIVE

David Wheeler, Director of the recruitment website 'Start in TV', sees acquiring work experience as essential, particularly in the media and creative sectors. *'You need to show that you're prepared to get your hands dirty and that you will use it as a chance to listen, observe and learn. A work placement or a job such as running is a sort of extended job interview – and, more often than not, you only get one chance. First impressions are important and, if you don't come up to scratch, you won't be asked back!'*

Sarah Walsh, Whitechapel Gallery

You may have already read Sarah's own story in Chapter 4 or seen what she has to say about the skills she looks for in a graduate in Chapter 2. Here's her take on job applicants.

Whitechapel Gallery is often swamped by CVs – a recent junior vacancy attracted about 1,000 applications. So what advice would Sarah give about marketing yourself?

'*We look for knowledge about the industry and about our gallery in particular. Generic CVs can't show this and are often discarded. And it's importance to give evidence for anything you have done or any skills that you feel you have, rather than just stating these as a fact.*' *A lot of graduates with artistic aptitude think that spending time on a highly coloured or original CV (sometimes called a 'stunt' CV) will pay dividends.* In Sarah's experience '*These rarely work and are often counterproductive. We've had what are almost full-scale art installations sent to us when what we need is a solid basic document – no gimmicks!*'

Sarah strongly suggests that you do a personal audit (of skills, interests, values, knowledge, aspirations) before producing a CV or contacting organisations. '*If you're sure of what you want to do and why, you become more attractive to employers.*'

Where and how does she suggest that you build up information about working in the arts? '*Get yourself on mailing lists such as ECCA, Artquest and the Arts Council mail shots. Read publications related to your area of interest. Attend events and training. Wherever you're aiming, just be sure that you understand how your industry functions: if you want to be employed by a gallery or an art dealer, find out about a whole range of organisations in that field, so that you can see how it all slots together.'*

Sarah also recommends doing some research on the financial structures that underpin the sector. You may not need to be a financial whiz kid, but it is vital to have an awareness of funding – bidding for funds from bodies such as the Arts Council is a major part of any art administrator's work – and on how sponsors are found and fundraising activities are carried out. Finally, she endorses 'schmoozing', an essential skill for all job hunters, especially those in the arts. This can be loosely summed up as: *'Go to events, make yourself seen, talk to people, build up contacts.'* Schmoozing is, in itself, a valid form of networking and jobs have been found in this way!

For more tips from Sarah, see the case study referred to above.

BE AHEAD OF THE CROWD

We've already extolled the virtues of networking, but being creative with your job hunting could also include speculative applications (don't wait for a job to be advertised). Contact the company direct with a strong CV and covering letter, which are tailored to the organisation's needs and which show that you have done your background research. Be prepared to 'chase' the CV by phone if you don't get a response in a fortnight or so.

There is also called cold calling and this isn't for the faint hearted. It involves phoning, emailing or going round in person and asking if there are any opportunities for a recent graduate like yourself. This technique is most commonly used in the creative arts and media sectors and is a valid way of finding work or placements. Take a business card, CV and some relevant examples of your work with you if you do decide to tread the pavements. Yes, you will find some doors slammed in your face, but you'll also get a foot inside others.

16 Resources

GENERAL

www.bbc.co.uk – information on careers in film and TV, in writing, in the performing arts and in design
www.businesslink.gov.uk
www.companieshouse.gov.uk
www.britishcouncil.org/erasmus
www.hecsu.ac.uk
www.hesa.ac.uk
www.ncge.com – the National Council for Graduate Entrepreneurship
www.prospects.ac.uk – careers information on all the career areas in this book and more!

CHAPTER 3

www.cilip.org.uk – Chartered Institute of Library and Information Professionals

CHAPTER 4

www.csd.org.uk – Chartered Society of Designers
www.dandad.org.uk

CHAPTER 5

www.civilservice.gov.uk

CHAPTER 6

www.startinTV.com
www.skillset.org
www.nctj.com

CHAPTER 7

www.mountbatten.org

CHAPTER 8

www.aah.org.uk – Association of Art Historians

CHAPTER 9

www.itt.co.uk – Institute of Travel and Tourism

CHAPTER 10

www.barcouncil.org.uk
www.iol.org.uk – Institute of Linguists
www.lawcareers.net

CHAPTERS 11 AND 12

www.palatine.ac.uk – site contains employability briefings for
music and performing arts

CHAPTER 14

www.tda.gov.uk – Training and Development Agency for
Schools – everything you need to know about teaching in
the primary and secondary sectors

CHAPTER 15

www.artquest.org.uk
www.careers-creative-living.co.uk – University of the Arts
careers site
www.careers.lon.ac.uk – The Careers Group, University of
London
www.ecca-london.org